Footsteps

Tales for the journey

Althea Hayton

Wren Publications

First published in 2014
by Wren Publications
PO Box 396
St Albans
Hertfordshire
England
AL3 6BE

www.wrenpublications.co.uk

Copyright © Althea Hayton

ISBN 978-0-9557808-7-5

All rights reserved. No part of this publication may be reproduced or transmitted in any form or by means electronic, digital or manual, including photocopying, recording or any other information storage or retrieval system, without the prior written consent of the publisher.

Chapter images © 2014 Jenni Beal Geddes

Cover photograph © 2014 Ortrun Benz

Printed and bound in UK and USA by
Lightning Source:

Lightning Source Inc. (US)
1246 Heil Quaker Blvd.,
La Vergne, TN, USA 37086

Lightning Source UK Ltd.
Chapter House, Pitfield, Kiln Farm,
Milton Keynes, MK11 3LW, UK

For John, who is my husband and my best friend

Contents

PART ONE : The journey begins   1

Landfall   3

Tim and Tom   9

Shira: The race   11

Shira: The forest   19

Shira: Into the mist   27

The storm   33

The clear stream   37

The parcel of dreams   40

PART TWO: Blocks to healing   44

Tiny's castle   47

The bridge of simplicity   55

Caterpillar   57

The bowl   64

The square man   69

The case   72

The coat   77

The dance   83

The jewel   87

Contents

Sam's garden	103
The store	109
The sailor	113
PART THREE : Healing steps	119
A pair of moccasins	121
The empty box	123
Orthan's herd	125
Hiding in the light	135
Sisyphus unbound	139
The door	145
The key	151
Beyond the wire	157
Out of the box	161

Other books by Althea Hayton

The Food Addicts Diet (as Tish Hayton)

Two Little Birds

A Healing Path For Womb Twin Survivors

Womb Twin Survivors: the lost twin in the Dream of the Womb

A Silent Cry: Womb twin Survivors tell their Stories

Untwinned: Perspectives on the Death of a Twin before birth

Food and You: Introducing the Four Zero Experience

Not out of Mind

The Silver Bird

Prayer in Pregnancy

Lucy's Baby Brother

The Food Addicts Diet

E-books

The Lonely Halo: How a young family coped when Mummy died.
Prayer after Abortion - A report of a day conference
Food and You: A brief introduction
Could YOU be a womb twin survivor?
Womb Twin Survivors -a brief review
Poetry for Womb Twin Survivors
Is your child a womb twin survivor?
You might be a womb twin survivor if...
Ripples from the womb - a manual for therapists
Camino Tales

FROM THE AUTHOR

These stories are allegories of personal growth. They came into my mind piecemeal, over the space of twenty years, including a time when I was writing and working as a counsellor, and later when I went on pilgrimage to Santiago de Compostela. Only recently, when I gathered all the stories together, did it occur to me that the entire set of more than thirty allegories describes a series of steps on the way to personal growth, healing or spiritual development - whichever way you wish to look at it.

The footsteps will guide you from a sense of lost-ness to a place of autonomy and positive action. There are three sets of stories: the first describes some of the places where you may find yourself when you first decide to make changes in your life. The second describes some of the common problems that will probably arise as you continue along the path. The third set describes what can be the final stages, where all resistance is set aside and growth to your maximum potential is welcomed and fully allowed. The metaphors are simple, but the allegories are profound. They are intended to provide fresh insights about some of the stages that are commonly reached during the healing process.

I hope you will find yourself in these stories and they articulate the way you feel sometimes. That can help. Every story in this book has a positive outcome, demonstrating how each stage can be navigated to the maximum good effect. I wish you well on your journey.

Althea Hayton
St Albans, 2014

Part One

First steps

Landfall

The first step on the journey is to become aware of the possibility of a better life. The awareness comes slowly, but gradually the changes come.

I was safe in that place. I knew where I was and what was going on. I was king of this little kingdom.

I was waiting but I didn't know what I was waiting for. The days proceeded predictably as I grew stronger, but I did not know what I was growing for. Then I was afraid because everything was changing. There was nothing I could do to stop it. I tried to brake the progress but I was not strong enough. I was suddenly catapulted out to a wide and immense universe and a great storm was raging there. I was in a little, vulnerable boat and it creaked and strained to stay afloat in the enormous waves. I clung to the sides, paralysed and unable to see clearly. I was completely helpless and afraid.

The storm sometimes abated and I was able to make things fast, so that when the great storms came again, I would be ready. The storms came at a time I could not predict but I was ready for them. I closed my eyes and held my breath and stayed still until they passed. So it went on for many, many years. I got used to the storms and my little boat; it was not much but it was mine and I was the captain.

Then a wave came and smashed the little boat so I was thrown into the sea. I grabbed hold of some passing wreckage and held on for dear life. In that terrible place was total desolation. I knew my vulnerability and again I was afraid.

I made a raft out of the wreckage and climbed onto it. Gradually, I became aware of a dim figure who was always very near but just out of sight. I never saw who it was but when he was near, things felt better and I felt more able to cope.

I felt this figure gently guiding me. I was so lost I did not know where I was to turn or what to do. The guide seemed to be steering the raft, so I clung on with my eyes closed. Then the guide, who I never saw, spoke to me.

"Steer the raft, and paddle it to the shore."

I was angry for he did not seem to understand that I did not know of any shore or even what a "shore" may be. All my life, the whole world had been only the sea and the storm.

Again and again the voice said, "Paddle your raft to the shore." It sounded kind and helpful.

Because I did not know what to believe or think, I decided to follow these instructions. I paddled and paddled but soon I saw that this was only taking me in circles. I knew I needed a rudder.

So I lifted out of the water a short wooden spar, which had always floated along with me but was not strong enough to be part of my raft. I used it for a rudder, so I could at least steer a straight course. With my rudder keeping me on course, I was heading somewhere - but I did not know where.

With a new focus to my energy, I paddled busily but there was always fog all around me. I paddled and paddled until my arms ached and I was light-headed with fatigue.

"Rest!" said the voice.

"No!" I cried. "I must keep paddling because I am heading - I don't know where. It is the meaning and purpose of my life. I will not rest!"

So I closed my ears to the voice. I paddled on, until finally I could do no more. I collapsed and said to the voice, "I cannot do any more - you take over."

In a coma of absolute exhaustion, I slept. The rest I so badly needed came to me at last. I dreamed of a place with images of brightness and creativity in a land I knew nothing of.

I awoke and became aware once again of the fog and the water, but the water was calmer and the waves less strong. So I took up my paddle once again and set my faithful rudder for a straight course. I paddled my little raft in the direction I thought was right. After many days and years, I found myself still in the place where I had always been.

I looked at the waves racing past me and it seemed as though I was progressing, but there were rocks beside me and they were always the same rocks. I worked hard to avoid them. I was afraid of the rocks, lest my little raft crash upon them and splinter into nothingness.

Then the voice whispered, deep in my heart, "Stop paddling and drift with the waves."

I was afraid, for if I stopped padding then I would be taken where I did not want to go. However, through the years I had learned to trust in the good intentions of this kindly voice, so I stopped paddling and let go.

At once I moved, but in the opposite way to the way I was trying to go. The current was taking me back and back to some place of long ago.

In that moment, it came clear to me that there was a tide - a current that was carrying me along. I learned to look at the water as I floated along, effortlessly. It felt good. I was being carried along by forces I did not understand, but it was so much better than the terrible hard work of trying to get somewhere in the sea and the fog.

So I took the leisure to look about me. I began to see shapes and forms emerging out of the fog. I learned that there was something other than endless sea.

I realised that there was another kind of place to be, that was not cold or wet. As I drifted slowly along I learned to see trees and grassy banks. The boat drifted slower and slower until it came to rest in the shallows. Still water lay about me.

Then I heard the strangest instruction of all, "Let go of the raft."

I was very afraid, for I was being asked to let go of everything safe. Yet the voice insisted, "Let go, and swim!"

I did not know that I could swim. I had always thought that I would drown if I did not have the wreckage of my former life to cling to. However, the raft began to disintegrate and I knew I must learn to swim. So I did. I swam and swam until I felt that I must drown, because I could not swim any more.

The voice came again, full of love. It said, "Now stand up and walk." I cried out, weeping, that if I stood up I would sink. I would never live to see the new life I was beginning to imagine for myself, there among the trees. I was almost dead with exhaustion, but tentatively I put my feet down. At once I felt firmness under my feet.

I touched it with my toes and recognised that it could bear my weight. Slowly, I inched forward. After a long time of terror of drowning, I was able to see clearly that there was land ahead.

Here was a dry place to stand, which I had only dreamed of but had never truly known. With the voice to guide me, I came to shore and dry land. I fell on my face with joy and gratitude.

After a long time of resting and recovery, I looked about me and saw that I was surrounded by dense fog. I explored a little, for I had learned to stand and also to walk my own path.

I looked back, to see that it was a river in which I had been swimming, against the current. Its clear and shallow water was sweet and good for swimming. In my joy, I leapt into the river once more, no longer afraid. I swam and capered in the waters, shouting and singing.

But the best times were when I came out of the water and stood tall and safe, upon the land.

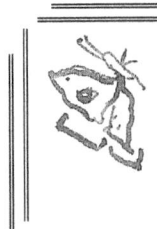 # Tim and Tom

The path of spiritual growth can be difficult and it is important not to escape into dreams....

Tim and Tom set out on a journey. Tim was a very determined man who walked straight and knew his destination. He just kept on going till he got there. But Tom was a dreamer, a romantic. He kept looking down the side turnings and saying, "Oh! Look at that wonderful waterfall! Look at that butterfly! I must go down there and see what that is like!"

But Tim said, "Come on - we must get on. Don't go off down all these side turnings!" And Tom just had to pass by and dream about what those side turnings might have meant. They walked along together for quite some time but Tom became increasingly unhappy. Eventually, he decided on one particularly beautiful mountain path, that stretched out around a fascinating and mysterious bend, with beautiful green trees overlooking it. He thought, "This one I have got to go for!"

So he said goodbye to Tim and set off down the mountain path. Tim kept on going. He walked through the heat and he walked though the rain. As he walked, he prayed. As he prayed, he grew stronger. As he walked along, he thought about Tim and he wondered where he was.

At the end of the road, when Tim arrived, he was amazed to find that Tom was already there. "Hi, Tim!" said Tom. "I've been waiting for you for two days."

Tim said, "Really? That's amazing!"

"Yes," said Tom. "The path that I took was a short cut. It got me here in no time at all."

Then they both knew what had happened. In his desire to explore and have fun and satisfy his dreams, Tom had missed the journey.

Shira - the race

The pursuit of happiness can take many forms. In this story, the pursuit is a headlong dash, with no thought for the consequences.....

A long time ago in a land far away, lived two brothers, Bara and Bild. They were strong and full of youth and energy for life. Bara was very tall, with deep, blue eyes that could see a speck on the horizon. Bild was so strong that he could lift great rocks and hurl them down the mountainside, to roll down into the river.

The two brothers lived to ride. They had horses, many of them, each with strong, muscular legs that would take them racing over the hills. They loved to race against each other. Sometimes Bild won and thrust his strong fist into the air with triumph, but his brother won just as often. Bara smiled until his blue eyes shone and he laughed with joy.

The races were longer and more arduous each time, as the brothers tested their skills against each other. Soon, there were no more mountains to conquer or deserts to cross.

So the two brothers went to their father and said, "Father, we have raced against each other over mountains and deserts and raging torrents, but this is not enough: we want to race the race of all races and see which of us is the finest horseman!"

The old man looked up at his tall sons and he was saddened, for they were both equally fine and strong and each was precious to him in his own way.

He thought for a long time and then he said, "There is one race that has never been won. There is one horse that is faster than any other - the greatest horse that ever lived. This is Shira. He has a flying golden mane and flashing black eyes and a tail like the west wind. Which of you will ride out in search of Shira?"

The two brothers spoke with one voice, "Let me go, Father!"

They knew that the one who caught Shira would have to ride faster than anyone else in the world ever did. After some argument between them, it was decided that they should go together. They each took the strongest horse they could find.

Bara took a strong black stallion called Tamba and Bild took a young mare called Mara, who he knew was very fast. Bara's sharp eyes would tell them where to go, while Bild's strength would drive them on.

So the two brothers raced onward and onward, night and day, to catch Shira, the fastest horse that ever lived. Sometimes they saw each other: at one time Bara was in front, at another it was Bild who was in the lead. They rode on and on, never tiring, in tune with their horses, exhilarated with the race. When the time came to rest, they snatched a brief time to feed Tamba and Mara and themselves, only to leap once more onto their horses and ride on.

Then the arguments started:

"When we find Shira I will ride him because I am the oldest!" said Bara.

"I am the strongest and will find Shira first: try and catch me!" cried Bild and he spurred his horse onward and onward, deep into the forest, until he could no longer see his brother.

In a clearing in the forest, Bild came across an old man standing by the path. The old man was holding a small wrapped parcel in his hand, and he reached out to Bild. "Stop!" he cried.

"I can't stop," cried Bild. "I have to catch Shira, the finest horse that ever lived!" I was king of this little kingdom.

He galloped onwards, the wind in his ears drowning out the

faint sound of the man calling after him. The old man looked sad, because in his parcel was the gift of discernment. This young man, flying through the forest, was going to need it in his search.

At the foot of a hill, Bild saw the slight, hooded figure of a woman standing in the centre of the path. Her head was bowed and wrapped in a fine, white cloth. He could not see her face. Bild steered his course around the woman, ignoring her. As he passed he thought he heard her soft, low voice singing, but maybe it was the sound of the west wind blowing. He galloped onwards, up to the brow of the hill where he would be able to see the horizon.

The woman raised her pale face as he passed. Her face was very beautiful and filled with pity. She gazed after Bild as he and his horse galloped away. Her dark eyes were filled with tears.

On the hilltop Bild gazed out over the plain below him. He was really worried. He hadn't caught a glimpse of his brother for some time and they both must be very near to Shira! He looked out over the forest as far as his eyes could see, searching for some sign of the magical horse, but there was nothing.

He knew Shira was out there, if only he could catch him! He knew that the horse was the purest white with a glowing, golden mane, flashing black eyes and a golden tail like the west wind. He set off once again at a gallop, down into the valley, dreaming of Shira. He knew that Shira was the greatest horse that ever lived. He imagined the strong, muscular flanks and the wide nostrils. In his heart he longed to see this wondrous horse!

For a moment he missed Bara's sharp eyes, for Bara would

surely be able to see into the deep forest for signs of that golden mane. Yet the thought that Bara may have spotted Shira already, filled him with even more urgency. He spurred his horse onwards, into the forest.

There was a sudden cry and Bild realised he had hit something. It was a little child, who lay at the side of the road, crying as he passed.

"Stupid child!" cried Bild. "I am after Shira and I have no time for you. You should not have got in the way!" and he rode on. The child sat up, rubbing his legs where they were injured. The child stared silently and sadly after Bild until he was a speck on the horizon, darting out of the forest and over the distant hill.

Bild was elated. He could not see his brother and surely that was because Bild was ahead! He would get there first; he would claim Shira for his own and be the world champion horseman!

There was a small ravine ahead. He steered his horse towards it and recklessly went into the jump. But something was wrong! The horse missed her footing. Instead of landing firmly on the other side, she slipped and slithered until the ground gave way. Horse and rider slid down into the ravine to the river below.

Fortunately, there were mosses and ferns growing there that broke their fall, but Bild was badly bruised and his horse was hardly able to move. He lay there weeping. The race was over for him and his horse. Shira would now be out of reach.

As he wiped away his tears, Bild realised how tired he was. He had not slept for many days and nights. He nursed his bruises and took a drink from the cool stream that ran through the ravine. Then, looking at his horse Mara, lying panting and sweat-covered beside him, he realised that she too was hurt and thirsty, but could not move to get a drink.

"Oh Mara! I have been cruel to you!" wept Bild, suddenly filled with remorse. He dragged Mara to her feet and led her gently to the river. Man and horse stood side by side. Mara drank, hung her head and just stood there, panting with exhaustion.

Bild felt so, so tired. He had never felt so tired before. He sank down to his knees and then lay there on the moss, among the ferns, and slept a deep, deep sleep. In the morning, he would make a plan to get out. Both horse and man slept all that day and through the night.

The next day, they set off slowly along the river to find a place where they could climb out of the ravine. To save his horse, Bild walked beside her and let her feed where she wanted. Bild was filled with a soul-deep weariness. Nothing was easy any more: there was no elation, no striving, no race to be won. No Shira.

Bild lay his head on his horse's smooth neck and slow tears of sorrow rolled down his face. Mara stood very still, her ears pricked forward, listening. Bild began to sob. He wept for the loss of his wild life, filled with the wind in his ears and the feel of Mara's strong movements under him, driving him on.

He wondered about the old man he had seen and what he had been holding in his hand. He wished he had stopped to talk to the old man. He wondered if the woman was beautiful and if she would have spoken to him if he had stopped to listen to her. He wondered if the young boy was badly injured and wished he had gone back to tend his hurts.

Bild had never felt so lonely or so sad. He knew that if he could not hunt for Shira, he had no reason for living. He knew that only the very strongest rider could catch Shira. But why had no one ever caught Shira? Why was this horse so elusive, as if the faster you rode to catch up, the faster he moved away?

Bild sat down to ponder on this at the riverside, his horse grazing contentedly by him. He watched the water moving its slow and thoughtful way along. He sat there for many hours until the sun went down and darkness fell. His heart was filled with sadness and longing for Shira.

He slowly realised that he would never catch Shira. All there would ever be was the race. He lay down upon the dewy grass and dreamed of Shira. In his dream the golden mane tickled his neck. He reached up his hand to feel the soft mane just there, behind his head. He stroked it gently, filled with deep contentment. Shira was there beside him. There was no need to race onwards and onwards. He could just be there, knowing Shira was near.

He opened his eyes and looked up. There was the golden mane, the long white nose! He leaped up in surprise. The huge horse turned and darted away into the dawn light. In a moment the vision was gone. Bild sat there for a moment, blinking. The dream had felt so real, but of course it was only a dream.

Then he set off again along the river. Slowly, as Mara recovered her strength, he rode her a little as the ravine widened. He began to look about him and enjoy the gentle ride. The sky was lightening towards a new day and he felt a deep contentment. He stopped his horse to gaze about him at the ravine, which was his prison with high walls, yet it was beautiful and filled with life in all its richness. Mara seemed restless and moved under him.

He looked back at the way he had come. There, among the trees, was a glimpse of a huge white horse with a flying golden mane. He rubbed his eyes in disbelief. Surely Shira was far away, out of reach of even the fastest horseman?

He turned away, his thoughts focussed upon the end of his journey out of the ravine. He urged Mara to go on a little faster but she seemed reluctant to hurry. Yet every time he looked back or around him, there was a spark of gold just visible through the trees, or the flash of a white flank in his eye corner.

Gradually, he came to believe that Shira might be there, just out of sight. At night, when Bild lay silent and still, Shira came closest. Then Bild could feel the soft mane and gentle breath on him. At dawn on the third day, he saw a valley open to the East and he knew that this was his way out of the ravine. He rode onwards and upwards onto the hilltop and looked out for a long time over the forest and the hills.

Then he knew for certain: he had been running after Shira and all the time Shira was behind him! He had been riding so fast that Shira couldn't catch him. He had been running away from Shira!

In that dark moment, he let go a wail of unimaginable sorrow...

 # Shira - the forest

Some people pursue happiness as an obsession of the mind, regardless of the pain that may be caused....

 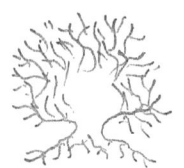

Meanwhile, Bara had been racing through the forest. Not for him the wild open spaces that Bild needed for this race! Bara had the eyes of a hawk and the ability to weave and skim though the trees and along the paths, faster than anyone. He searched out with his keen sight a faint pathway, where few had walked before. Boldly he took it, spurring Tamba onwards and onwards to run faster and faster.

Bara kept his eyes fixed upon the darkest places in the forest, for he knew that somewhere in the hidden depths of the forest was the place where Shira lived. If such a wonderful white horse with a golden mane were to be out there in the open, then surely the whole world would already know him and be able to see him! No. Bara was sure, with his keen mind and clear eyes of deepest blue, that only the keenest sight and sharpest wit would be able to locate the hidden place where Shira would be found.

In his secret heart, Bara was a proud man and was fiercely jealous of his brother's enormous strength. To win the race, he had to believe that his eyes were the keenest and his mind the sharpest. He worked hard to use his eyes to read the signs of Shira's passing and use his wits to deduce where he may be hiding. His only thought was that secret hiding place.

He saw a hoof-print upon the ground and stopped his horse to examine it carefully. He placed his own foot into the print and wondered at the size of it. He spent some time there, staring at the shape in the ground. It pointed towards a dark place in the trees, showing him the way.

Out of the corner of his eye he spotted a small figure of a man wearing a cloak the colour of autumn leaves.

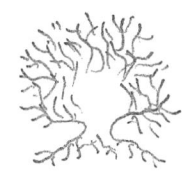 

Curious, and not wanting to miss a single clue, Bara slowed his pace and approached the man. He had a kindly face, but Bara did not know who he was and if he would be wise enough to help him. The man said nothing but handed Bara a crumpled piece of paper and then melted into the woods out of sight.

Bara opened the paper and saw that it was a map. It was filled with strange signs. It was hard to understand. Bara spent a long time trying to work out which way he was to go. It seemed that where he was in the forest was not on this map. Maybe he was looking in the wrong place! Suddenly afraid that he had made a terrible mistake, Bara decided to see if he could find the edge of the forest, so that he might be able to find where he was on the map.

Staring into the distance, he tried to guess which way was perhaps a little lighter, where the sun was showing through the trees. He kept to a slow pace, and stared and stared ahead of him, seeking out any slight changes in the intensity of the light. He knew that if he lost his way in the woods, he would lose the race altogether. But for Bara in that moment, the race was less important than finding out where he was on the map.

As he fixed his eyes on the distant glimmer through the trees, again and again Bara ripped his clothes upon brambles and briars. Tamba was scratched and bleeding along his flanks, yet Bara did not stop to stem the flow of blood on his own legs or tend the wounds of his horse. As the day wore on and the night fell, both horse and rider stumbled more and more, until the pain became too hard to bear. It was time for Bara to rest and tend his wounds and staunch the blood that now flowed freely from the

 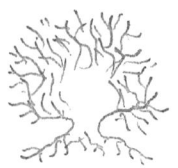

flanks of his faithful black stallion.

He dismounted, stiff and sore from the long ride, and bound up his own wounds. Then he looked at his horse, who stood there with his deep, dark eyes filled with loyalty and readiness to carry Bara as far as he wished. Bara felt remorse for how roughly he had treated his beautiful horse. He had chosen Tamba for the race and he had carried him strongly and well. Bara had relied on him totally.

Gently he took moss from the ground around the trees. Speaking softly, he placed the moss along the horse's flanks, took him to a small stream to drink and let him graze freely upon the soft forest undergrowth. Gradually the look of pain in his horse's eyes began to fade and he came to stand by Bara, who was resting against a tree. Then Bara slept, tired, weary and lost in the dark wood. He dreamed of Shira's magical kingdom in the hidden heart of the woods. Sometimes it felt as if Bara was already there, with Shira near him.

For many days, Bara wandered in the forest. At each crossroads he waited for a long, long time. He thought as hard as he could and he looked as far as he could, until his mind was in a whirl and his eyes ached. It felt as if there had never been a time when he was not lost among these trees, with only the occasional glimpses of sun to tell him the time of day.

But as the forest grew darker, it felt as if, after all, they were approaching the hidden place where Shira lived. Bara had to choose between finding the way out of the forest, to see where he was on the map, and exploring deeper into the forest to find Shira's hiding place. He decided to risk going deeper. The strange

feeling in his heart, that Shira was very near, had been deepening every day.

It became so dark in the forest that he had to rely upon his ears more than his eyes. The trees were tall and mysterious. They spoke to him in a language he did not understand. In the high winds, the trees creaked and the wind screamed. He was too afraid to listen and put his hands over his ears. Later, in the soft, gentle breezes, there was a whisper that he never quite heard or understood, however hard he tried.

The darkness became deeper and the trees were so close together that there was only room to crawl through. It was time to leave Tamba to find his own way out of the forest and graze the wide green meadows, if he could.

Bara made his farewell to his faithful stallion and wished him well. Then slowly and gingerly, for there were many sharp thorns, he plunged into the undergrowth, with his heart and mind fixed upon his dream of the magical place in the depths of the wood. There in the centre of the forest, Bara would find the wonderful white horse Shira, with his golden mane and tail and wise black eyes!

Bara soon reached an open space and began to imagine that he knew the way. He set off surefooted, fighting through the low branches, sweeping away the nettles with his feet, until eventually he became exhausted. He came to a stop and fell to his knees. He was lost. He had been lost for a very long time.

He was alone and hungry. He found berries to eat, growing there in the forest. Sometimes they tasted bitter but he ate them sooner than starve, for he knew he needed strength to carry on -

 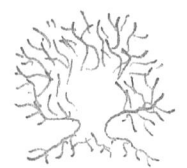

to keep trying. He knew, if he only kept believing, that one day he would find the way to the magical place that he now yearned for constantly.

The next day he awoke from his bed of soft leaves. He was glad to see that the sky was still visible above him and the daylight was coming with the dawn. Filled with fresh hope, he walked the long and lonely path that lay ahead, sometimes looking back to where he had been, sometimes searching through the trees for some sign that another person had passed the same way, to reassure him that he was following the right path.

If he kept his eyes on the ground he was occasionally able to see footprints, sometimes facing forwards, sometimes seeming to retreat the way he had come. He found it reassuring that others had been there before him, but clearly they too did not know the way out.

If he kept his eyes on the sky above, he often got the feeling that there was someone with him, but always when he looked round there was no one there. When that happened he grieved a little, for he craved company and support in his long, endless journey. It seemed so hard to make it on his own. He tried not to think about that and relied upon himself, his own eyes and his own ability to find his way.

Soon he wept tears of hunger. He yearned to be fed. He realised that after all, his eyes were not sharp enough to see and his wits were not clever enough to discover the magical hiding place where Shira was to be found. He longed for the safety and certainty of home.

It did not seem important any longer that Bild had certainly

won the race and Bara would be the loser. It mattered only that he was lost. He knew that if he did not find food, he would be unable to continue his long and arduous journey.

Eventually, he became so weak he was unable to walk another step. He sank down onto a pile of soft leaves and wept, for he knew that he had no more strength to journey on and must therefore always be lost. Yet in the dark night of weeping he felt a gentle touch and dared to feel strength and hope grow in him. After that, he remained hungry but he had hope. This was enough for him to continue.

So he went on, filled with hope, wondering whose touch it was that he had felt, so gentle upon his shoulder. Every night he felt it upon him but he dared not look, for fear that it would fade and be gone. So in his mind he asked the giver of that touch to remain there upon his shoulder, for surely he did not need food so much as guidance.

If this reassuring presence would only guide him, then he could find his way home. So he closed his eyes and let the presence guide him. As he stumbled onwards, he did not know if he was turning this way or that. The journey was long and difficult and sometimes he wanted to open his eyes to save himself if he stumbled on a tree root, but somehow the presence held him enough to prevent him falling.

He grew impatient. He wanted to know if he had arrived at the edge of the forest, where once again he would be able to use his eyes and wits to find his way home. Yet in his heart he knew that he must continue to wait and trust in his guide, until he felt the sun warm upon him once again. He walked slowly, step by

 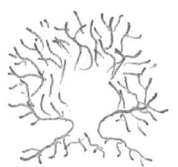

step, on and on.

He knew that he would never have been able to find his way without this gentle guide to help him. How had he ever imagined that he could get out of the woods simply by trial and error, experimenting randomly with this or that path!

In the darkness, his blue, long-sighted eyes closed, relying totally upon the guide, he soon felt a deep sense of rightness, that this was the right path. It was not smooth but pitted with holes and barred by branches and briars that whipped his skin and drew blood as he passed. But he kept trust in his guide.

For some time after that, in the whispering breeze, he could hear soft and loving voices speaking to him, but he did not know what they were saying.

Suddenly he felt a change in the wind. In the scream of a gale, Bara heard a wail of unimaginable sorrow...

Shira - into the mist

The pathway to spiritual growth is mysterious and the end result always surprising. Trust in the process.....

The wailing cry echoed around the tall trees. At once, Bara turned his step towards the sound, for he wanted to find out who was so filled with sorrow. He wondered if he could help this person in their pain. Meanwhile, the loving voices became stronger and stronger. He knew then that, if he was truly going to help this poor wretch, he must open his eyes. So he did.

There before him was Bild, weeping at the side of his mare, Mara. Bara raced towards his brother, to embrace him and give him all the love he could muster.

"I have found Shira", said Bild, sadly.

Bara was puzzled. "Then if this is true, why are you weeping? Why do you look so sad?"

Bild told him the story of how he had found Shira, but not in the race; that Shira was always with him, nearby but just out of sight.

Bara caught his breath. "But that is just what I have found!" he cried. He looked around then for his guide, so that he could see his face and thank him for guiding him to this place, for the trees were thinning now and Bara could see the way clearly into the light. But there was no guiding touch upon his shoulder; no gentle presence beside him. There was no one there.

Bara understood then why Bild was weeping. His own heart was breaking because he would never find Shira's magical hiding place and now even that loving, guiding presence was gone.

The two brothers sat together at the edge of the forest with Mara grazing nearby. They silently grieved for all their dreams: for the race that could never be; for the unattainable Shira; for the elusive, magical place that would never be found.

For a long time they tried to comfort one another. Then their hearts lifted a little, for Tamba came towards them from out of the forest. They took that as a sign to get going again and try to find their way home.

So the two brothers mounted their horses and set off along a well-worn path on their way out of the forest. Sometimes Bild caught a glimpse of a golden mane, just out of sight. When the darkness fell, Bara had a strong sense of a guiding touch but it faded when he awoke the next day. Bild too had known the soft touch in his dreams. They both learned to recognise that this was Shira.

It was a long, long journey. They did not seem to be getting anywhere that Bara could recognise on the map, despite his close and regular scrutiny of every possible path. Bara scanned the horizon and thought as hard as he could and Bild summoned up all his strength to endure, but to no avail.

One day they were sitting in a grassy clearing when Bild had an idea. "When you were lost in the forest and you walked with closed eyes, Shira guided you to the place where I was."

Bara had not thought about it in quite that way before. He said, "I suppose that was Shira, guiding me."

Bild went on: "And I often get a glimpse of his mane, just out of the corner of my eye, but it seems as if I never manage to see him properly."

"He is hiding from you," said Bara.

Bild turned to his brother. "But not from you."

Bara looked at Bild for a long time. His bright blue eyes shone with hope. His quick mind wondered what all this could

mean. Then he knew and his eyes darkened.

"He comes to me when my eyes are closed," he said. "When I am blind."

Bara had always had the gift of far-seeing and had come to rely on this gift. At that moment, he realised that to get home he must relinquish his far sight and rely on the gentle touch of the unseen, wonderful horse to guide him.

Bild had other ideas. If Shira came to Bara when his eyes were closed, then Bild would be able to see him properly, close to, in all his beauty! So Bild went and hid in the bushes while Bara waited with eyes closed. They waited for a long time, until they were weary with waiting, but the horse never came.

Then Bild said, "Perhaps Shira is hiding from me now. He seems to come when I least expect it."

"Yes," said Bara. "Maybe you need to close your eyes too."

So they roped the horses together and sat still, waiting, both with their eyes closed, both wishing that Shira would come so they could feel the soft guiding touch. Hours passed and there was nothing.

Soon they decided that they would have to move somehow. They set off slowly, with eyes closed, still roped together towards the setting sun.

They both had the feeling that Shira may be somewhere near but they were afraid to look, in case he disappeared. They moved slowly, neither of them knowing where they were going, but still there was no soft touch, no guide. Eventually they stopped in a green meadow where the horses began grazing greedily.

Bara began to laugh. "Of course we have arrived here in

this wonderful soft grass!" he cried. "We may have had our eyes closed but the horses knew exactly where they were going!"

Bild looked puzzled. "You mean that only if they too do not know where they are going that Shira will come? Is he is hiding from them too?"

Bara shrugged. "Maybe, who knows? Anyway, tomorrow I will bind up their eyes. Then we will all be unable to see and perhaps then Shira will come at last and guide us home!"

The next day they saddled up and bound the horses' eyes. Then Bara and Bild mounted their blind horses, closed their own eyes and waited for Shira to come and show them the way. They waited for a long time, but there was no soft touch to guide them, only the sound of a gentle breeze. They moved off slowly, still believing that if they waited long enough, Shira would come.

The gentle breeze became a strong wind at their back, almost blowing them along the path. Bild felt afraid but he relied upon his strength to give him courage. Bara was wondering why the breeze had become a strong wind so suddenly.

They blindly stumbled on and on, the horses picking their way slowly through the rocks. Bara soon became concerned for the horses, because there were so many rocks.

"I am going to unmask the horses," he said. "They may get hurt."

Opening his eyes he saw that they were in a thick mist and only a few feet in front of them was visible.

"Bild! You may as well open your eyes now, for we can't see where we are going anyway. There is a mist."

Bild opened his eyes and looked around him. There was no

sign of any familiar landmarks. They were totally lost. The rocky path was visible under their feet but it was not clear where it was going. The pathway was all they had to guide them. The sound of rushing water was somewhere near.

All at once, Bara knew what to do. "This is enough to go on!" he cried. "We have the pathway and the sound of the river, so let's go on, bit by bit. We are not lost if we have these."

So the two horses and their riders moved on into the mist, with the pathway and the river to guide them, heading towards home.

The Storm

The journey will bring pain to the surface and this will be difficult. There will always be choices about how to handle this......

Two friends, Martin and Mike, were walking along the road. A storm was brewing up behind them and they didn't know what to do. They had two choices: One was to run before the storm and get into some kind of shelter so they didn't get wet. The other was to turn round into the storm and walk through the rain so it would soon pass over.

Martin wanted to run before the storm and get into shelter before he felt any of that rain at all. But if he did that, he would have to run really, really fast.

So Martin turned to Mike and said, "I'm going to run really, really fast! I'm going to get to the shelter before the storm hits. I will stay dry and I will be safe."

So Martin ran on as fast as he possibly could. His feet began to hurt and his legs began to ache, but the storm was always just behind him and he could not stop.

He had to run virtually the whole of the day to avoid the storm, for the shelter was a long way away. Finally, he got to the shelter and hid there. He was absolutely exhausted but the storm passed over him and he stayed completely dry.

Mike decided that he would turn back and walk into the storm. Now this seemed to be crazy, but actually the storm was moving quite fast. So he walked into the storm and within half an hour the storm had passed him.

He was not exhausted and his legs were fine. He was very wet, but he had his raincoat on and he re-organised all his clothing. He turned round to face his destination and saw the clouds pass into the distance in front of him.

He walked on along the road once more. The sun came out,

THE STORM

the air was fresh and so was he. He walked on for the rest of the day, wondering how his friend had got on.

When he caught up with his friend at the end of the day, Mike felt fresh and bright but Martin felt exhausted and sad. They compared notes as to what to do, next time a storm came.

Would they run fast before it to stay safe and dry? Or would they turn and walk through it, so it would pass more quickly?

The Clear Stream

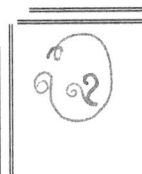 

The path to healing and spiritual growth begins well if there is a time of inner cleansing at an early stage....

There was a young man called Tristram who had been walking all day and he was very dusty and dirty. He came to a beautiful clear stream, and he asked the people around him, "What is the name of this stream?"

And the people said, "This is the River of Purity. Anyone who walks through the river will be cleansed."

So Tristram rushed into the river with his heart bursting with joy. Oh! This was where he was going to be cleansed!

He walked through the river and out the other side. All the dust was washed off his clothes and off his boots. He was very wet but he walked on into the sunshine. Gradually his clothes dried and he looked as good as new and fresh as the morning. As he was walking along, a Wise Man walked with him.

He said to the Wise Man, "Look! I have been cleaned in the River of Purity."

The Wise Man said, "No, you haven't."

Tristram said, "But I have! Look how clean my boots are! Look how clean my trousers are! There is not a speck of dust on me now."

The Wise Man said, "No. No you are not cleansed. You must turn and go back into the river."

Tristram looked defiant. "I'm not going to go back! I am on an important journey and I don't want to turn back."

The Wise Man said softly, "Well, it's your choice not to. However, if you do decide to turn back, when you walk through the river take off all your clothes, for your clothes are clean but your body is not."

Tristram stood stock still on the road. He didn't know what

to do. Would he walk on, in the hope of perhaps finding another river where he could take off his clothes and wash his body?

Or should he go back and think again how he should walk through the River of Purity?

The Wise Man walked on and Tristram stood uncertain on the way.

Then a young girl came along and walked up to him and took his hand. She said nothing to him but she pulled him back along the road, back to the place where he had walked through the river.

There were other people walking through the clear stream of the river. He saw that before they stepped into the river they took off all their clothes.

As naked as the day they were born, they went into the river and emerged, clean and fresh and new.

Tristram was smiling as he watched. He knew then what he must do.

The Parcel of Dreams

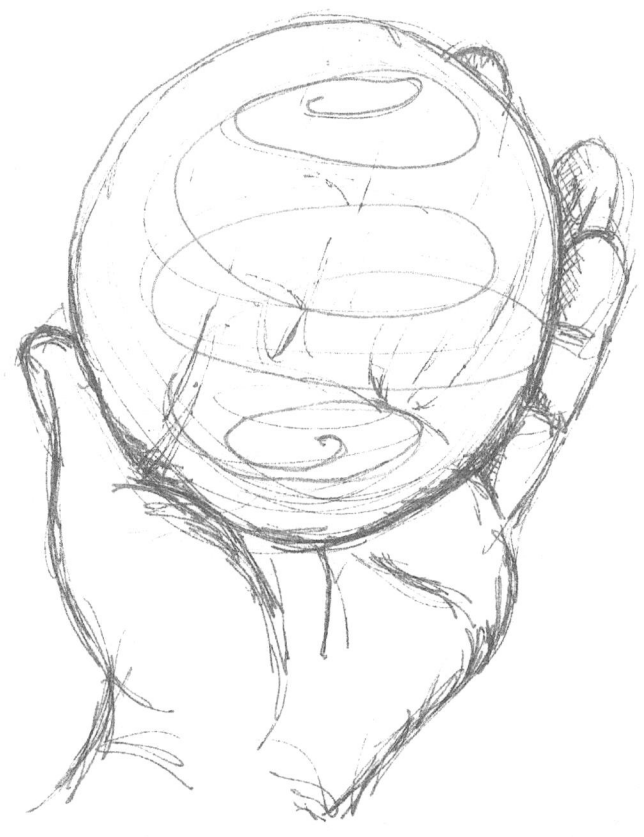

An important early step is to let go of impossible dreams, including dreams of how much healing or growth is actually possible...

There was a man called Almos who was walking through the world and he carried in his bag a parcel of dreams. It was a very light parcel and he loved it very much. When he was walking along, he looked into it and dreamed his dreams. They helped him to walk along the road.

One day, he reached a point in the journey where he came across the Dream Master. The Dream Master asked him to stop, so he stopped.

The Dream Master said, "Please, show me your parcel of dreams." Almos was a bit suspicious and didn't like the sound of this at all, but he did as the Dream Master said and opened the parcel.

The Dream Master said, "Show me your dreams."

So Almos took out his favourite dream, which was an iridescent bubble of joy and happiness. This was the dream that he didn't have to choose between two options - he could have both. When he made a choice, he could have both choices. He could have everything. He loved that dream so much!

And the Dream Master looked at the dream and he said, "Are you carrying your Sword of Truth?" Almos, because he was an honest man, carried his Sword of Truth everywhere. He said, "Yes, I have it here."

The Dream Master said, "I want you to plunge your Sword of Truth into the bubble of your dream." Almos was very afraid, because what would he do if his dream was burst? But he did as the Dream Master said and he plunged his Sword of Truth into the bubble of the dream.

The dream didn't burst, it just faded until it was gone. Then

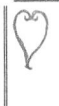 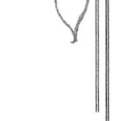

a great wave of joy and happiness filled his heart. He realised how much joy and happiness had been tied up in this beautiful, iridescent bubble that he had carried everywhere with him.

Then the Dream Master said, "Do you have another dream in your bag?" Almos pulled out another dream. It was dark, scarlet, warm and comforting. It was the dream that he could have it all. He could have it now and he wouldn't have to wait. The Dream Master said nothing.

Almos knew what he must do. With great courage, he took his Sword of Truth and plunged it into the dream. The dream gradually diminished until it had turned into a little pool of tears. Almos wept a little and then wiped his tears away. Now he was full of joy and happiness and his tears had been wiped away, but the Dream Master asked again, "Is there another dream in your bag?"

Almos was not sure. "I think so," he said, and felt right down in the bottom of his bag. There he found a little silver object. It was bright and it reflected the light. He took it out. It was small and he could hold it in his hand. The Dream Master said, "What dream is this?"

Almos said, "This is my dream of total healing - that I will be totally healed."

The Dream Master said, "Give me the dream."

Almos didn't understand. The Dream Master silently held out his hand. Almos handed his precious dream to the Dream Master. Then he understood. Now that he had given away his dream of total healing, it had become possible.

Part Two

Blocks to Healing

Tiny's Castle

The path to spiritual growth can be blocked by trauma, which can take a long time to overcome....

Once upon a time there was a king, who was very small. He was so small that other people called him Tiny but he was king nonetheless. King Tiny lived in a palace that wasn't so bad.

Then one day a war began. There was noise and terror and nothing seemed certain any more

Tiny summoned a band of men to build him a wall around the palace. Tiny and his friends stopped laughing and playing games and spent all their time building.

At first there was just a wooden palisade but the noise went on, so they made bricks and dug up stones from the ground nearby. Sometimes stones were thrown over the wall they were building but they did not have to be afraid - they just used them to make the walls thicker and higher.

Tiny was proud of his wall. He was sure it was the best wall in the world. "If we build it just a bit thicker and higher we won't be able to hear any noise at all!" he cried.

But that didn't work, so they decided to make their own noise. They shouted and screamed and jumped until they couldn't hear anything except their own noise. This was good! When there was lots of noise inside as well as out, they could feel safe, but at night, when there was no sound in the castle, Tiny could hear the enemy moving around outside. He imagined all the ways the enemy might get in, so he decided to make a castle keep, with a thick wall and tiny windows.

He worked so hard on building the castle keep, that he sometimes forgot about the war raging outside. He liked that. When the keep was built, the ground was bare and rutted because of the stones they had dug up. The clearing was not the

TINY'S CASTLE

beautiful lawn it had once been. Tiny often dreamed of how the lawn had once looked and how soft it had been to lie on. So he made cushions and built a warm fire. He and his men sat around the fire telling stories. When they did that, they couldn't hear the noise of the war outside.

For a long time it worked very well: whenever stones came over the wall, Tiny laughed to show he wasn't afraid and used the stones to make his castle stronger and stronger. He was king of his own castle and he was invincible!

One day, cannon balls came flying as the soldiers outside tried to batter down the walls. He summoned his men and made a long speech about courage and endurance. He felt very strong. There was nothing the enemy could do to get into his castle. Then Tiny decided to wear a crown, which made him feel special. He played all kinds of games with his men - which he won, of course, because he had made up all the rules.

The cannon balls kept on coming and Tiny had to admit he was feeling a bit afraid. He decided to mount a guard at the gate. He told his soldiers to be there night and day to keep the castle safe.

One day the baker came to him and said, "We need some more men to make bread."

"No!" said Tiny. "We need to keep the guard by the gate, in case the enemy breaks in." So the baker managed somehow. Anyway, Tiny knew he could manage without bread.

Then the jester came to him and said, "We need some more men to make up the team games. There can be no games if there aren't enough men."

"No!" said Tiny. "We must keep up the guard. Anyway, games are a waste of time; we must keep working if we are to make this castle truly safe."

So it went on: the guard at the gate got bigger and bigger until half the work force was on guard duty. Everyone was getting tired but Tiny was good at making speeches. He pranced and danced, telling his men how well they were doing.

"If we can survive this, we can survive anything! In fact, one day, when we get it just right, we may win the war!" Tiny shouted, in his most courageous voice. Tiny felt safe as long as he was making speeches, or prancing about or making his men laugh. But there was an uneasy feeling inside him that was asking to be expressed. He wondered: would they be able to keep the enemy away? Would they really have enough strength to resist if the enemy broke through? But he dared not admit this, because he knew that if his men felt frightened they wouldn't be able to do the work.

Then Tim, one of the children in the castle, came to him and said, "Please Your Majesty, the men are afraid."

"Afraid? What nonsense!" said Tiny at once. He rushed out and reassured his men harder than ever.

Tim was waiting for him in his room that night. "Please, Your Majesty, the men are angry. They want to decide what to do about the enemy."

King Tiny was very, very annoyed. He said, "How can I run this castle properly if there are people who disagree with me?" and he doubled the guard at the gate and got the others to polish up the dungeons.

TINY'S CASTLE

Then Tim came to him and said, "The guards want to look over the wall."

"No!" said Tiny. "We can't have that, for if they show their faces they will be shot. Tell them to keep their heads down!"

Tim persisted. "It has been many months now since any stones have come over the wall, and our keep needs repairing on the outside. What shall we do?"

The King was irritated by Tim's lack of respect for his authority but he knew in his inner heart that Tim was right. "Just use what you have," he said gruffly, "for it is essential that we keep the walls thick and strong." So the men took bits from here and there to repair the walls of the keep. Gradually they began to crumble again and Tiny noticed this. "Never mind," he thought to himself, "the outer wall is thick enough. We can stay safe inside the castle yard."

The soldiers on guard at the outer gate were getting old and tired. When King Tiny came out one day he found some of them asleep. "Wake up!" he cried. "Don't sleep on the job! The enemy might come!"

Something had to be done. "It is time for new guards!" cried Tiny, and he set about changing the guard. He replaced the old tired guards with bright new ones, who stood to attention at their posts and did not sleep. But they weren't like the old guards. They questioned why they had to stand there at attention all the time. They wanted to do shorter shifts.

King Tiny got very worried, but Tim, who had by this time become a firm friend, said, "Let's try it and see. Let's see if the enemy makes any more noise if we have fewer guards on duty."

Tiny listened and listened. The enemy was quiet. It seemed all right for the moment. So he kept his guards on alert but let them work shorter hours.

Then Tim said to King Tiny one day, "Why don't we look over the wall and see what the enemy is doing?" King Tiny was very frightened. "If we do that they will shoot us down!" he cried. But it seemed like a good idea, so he said, "Let's get prepared to take a look. Let's be ready with our tin helmets on and our guns loaded!"

Tim and King Tiny went into the meeting room in the depths of the castle and made detailed plans for what they would do when they looked over the wall. King Tiny tried to plan for every eventuality: what to do if the enemy soldiers were right under the walls, waiting in silence to pounce; what to do if they had guns trained on the walls, just waiting for someone to show up. The planning went on for a long time.

Then the day came when King Tiny decided it was time to look over the wall. He climbed up almost to the top of the wall several times, but when he got closer he was sure he heard the enemy waiting below, so he shouted and danced to scare them away, and decided to stay hidden.

One day he was wandering about near the outer wall, when he saw with dismay that there was a small hole where the stones had crumbled away, and daylight was shining through the wall. He put his nose close to the hole and peered through. He saw the plain stretching to the far distance. It looked peaceful and inviting. Just for a moment something in his heart opened, and a deep longing feeling erupted in his chest. He turned away, angry

TINY'S CASTLE

and sorrowful that he could not go out there. He was trapped inside the castle and could not get out.

After that day things changed. Tiny became obsessed with getting out of the castle. He dreamed about the day when he could step out and be free. Tim was the friend he needed, for he listened carefully, and stood by Tiny when he was feeling angry or sad. Then one day Tim said, "I have seen over the wall."

The King was very fearful then. "You have?"

"Yes. I looked over the wall and I am going to look again now. Coming?"

Tiny followed Tim to the upper battlements and watched from a lower step while Tim stood in the sun and gazed into the distance. Tiny ducked, waiting for the shot. None came.

"Come and look!" cried Tim.

"Maybe another time," whispered the King, feeling suddenly very small and weak. Then he summoned the guards one by one. "When you feel ready," he said, "please go and check over the wall to see if it is safe." And they did. One by one, they risked looking out and they remained alive. There was no shot.

"They are obviously waiting for me," thought Tiny. "Unless I too look out over the wall, I cannot declare the castle safe."

So he took another look though the hole and then found another, larger hole to look through. The endless plain was still there, calling him. It seemed safe, so he climbed the ladder with Tim beside him and quickly took a glimpse. The plain lay before him, a wide expanse of green, brown and blue.

For a terrible minute Tiny thought his heart would explode with longing and regret. He ducked down again, unable to stand it any longer. But the next day he was back. Now he had learned to look out, he wanted it more and more. The guards came up with him and they all looked out for a long time.

"It seems safe," said one of the soldiers, hesitantly. "Maybe we could go outside."

"Maybe," said Tiny.

Again Tim led the way, and he opened the gate and stood back. The guards stood either side of their king. Pulling himself up to his full height, Tiny stepped forward gingerly. The guards flanked him on each side as he walked. The gate loomed over them and they eventually stepped out into the green meadow beyond the walls.

There was no one there. No noise, not a soul about. They walked around for a while and then came back joyfully, but locked the gate against the enemy in the night. After that they went out each day. The guards were taken off the walls and came with their king to protect him. The enemy soldiers were nowhere to be seen and everything was quiet.

One day Tiny stood among the flowers in the meadow and looked back at the walls that he and his men had built. "I don't like those high walls!" he said. "I can't see this meadow from my window, so let's knock them down!"

The guards knocked down the walls and the castle keep was revealed. They made a big window in the wall so that the king could see out onto the plain. Then the guards made little houses for themselves out of the broken stones, for the king had little need of them now. He was busy exploring the land all around.

The Bridge of Simplicity

*The path to spiritual growth frequently involves letting go
and moving out of one's comfort zone...*

There was a man called Paulo and he was walking along the road. He came to a bridge and it crossed the River of Simplicity. If he could cross this river, he would be able to reach the Land of Simplicity that lay on the other side. As he approached, he noticed that the bridge had a gate. It seemed as if the gate was closed to him, until he got a little closer. Then he noticed that the gate was just wide enough to see through. He took a glimpse though the narrow opening and knew at once that he wanted to be through there. However, it was too narrow for him to get through.

So he went to the bridge keeper's house and he knocked on the door. He asked the bridge keeper what he should do. He said, "I want to get across the river to the Land of Simplicity on the other side but I can't get through the gate."

The bridge keeper smiled and said, "Perhaps, if you could cast off that big cloak that you are wearing to keep yourself warm, then you could get through the gap. I can't make the gap any wider. It is as wide as it must be. Each person must pass through it."

Paulo looked at the gap and thought, "There's no way I can pass through that!"

Then the bridge keeper took him into his house and he showed him a room full of cloaks that other people had cast off. Paulo understood. He took off his cloak and he laid it there, with so many other cloaks that had been laid there before him.

Only then could he pass easily through the gap and onto the bridge. Without his heavy cloak, he walked on with a lighter step, into the Land of Simplicity that lay on the other side.

Caterpillar

Some blocks to your spiritual growth and healing lie entirely in your imagination...

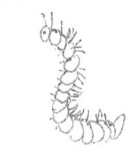

This is a story about two caterpillars, Clara and Carl, who lived in a garden long ago. Every day they wandered up and down the leafy stems and munched at the succulent leaves, and watched the butterflies landing lightly on a twig, folding their wings against the rain or opening them to the sun.

The two caterpillars did not have much to say to each other, for they were engaged in the process of eating, growing and becoming large enough to turn into butterflies. Their friendship was mostly a silent one, as they crawled and munched.

Carl wanted to become a truly wonderful butterfly. He often thought about the strong and wonderful painted wings he would have when he was changed in the magical chrysalis. Carl dreamed and dreamed until all he could see, all he could think about, were his dreams of his wonderful, painted wings. His dreams were clearer when he kept his eyes shut, so he often hung there, replete with leaves, sleeping and dreaming of better things.

Clara was ashamed of being a caterpillar. She felt fat and furry and hated the fact that she must crawl on the ground while the others were already butterflies, fluttering in the sunshine. She wanted so much to fly. She often dreamed about it. In her dream, she flew effortlessly into the sky, soaring and turning, visiting every flower in the garden.

She resented being a caterpillar so much. However much she ate, however hard she tried, she stayed a caterpillar. Every day she asked Carl to get out his magic mirror and she would look at herself in it. Sure enough, there she was - her own eyes and face but the body of a caterpillar behind them.

 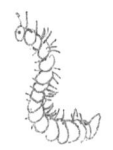

It continued for a long time. Carl dreamed of being the biggest and brightest butterfly in the garden and kept his eyes closed so that he could better see his dreams.

Every day, Clara begged Carl to show her his magic mirror, so that she could see if there were any signs of her changing. All the other caterpillars were changed into butterflies, but Clara and Carl were left still on the ground, munching and dreaming.

Then one day a grasshopper came and spoke to them. He saw Carl's magic mirror and he said, "Carl, may I look in our magic mirror?"

Clara and Carl let him look. The grasshopper stared and stared, as if he couldn't believe his eyes, and went off without saying anything.

Clara watched the grasshopper leaving them in such a hurry. She looked into the mirror to see if there was anything wrong with it, but sure enough there was the same face, the same eyes and the same caterpillar body.

Clara thought and thought about the grasshopper. She decided to ask him what he had seen that had made him leave in such a hurry.

She found him sitting by a still pond. "Grasshopper, what did you see in Carl's magic mirror that made you leave in such a hurry?" she asked. The grasshopper said nothing. He just stared into the still water of the pond. Clara waited patiently for him to reply, but still he said nothing.

Then she looked into the pond and saw herself. The same face, the same eyes - but there was something a bit different about her body. What was it? She looked closer. All along her

trunk there were thin stripes of varying colours, instead of the usual furry green. This made her feel afraid, because she was not sure what colour she was any more.

She went back and took a look in Carl's mirror and sure enough she was the usual furry green. This made her feel a bit better, but she wondered and wondered: which mirror was right? Were there stripes along her body, or was she furry green?

So she asked Carl: "Carl, what colour am I?"

Carl answered without opening his eyes, because he already knew, "You are a furry green. I am brown with yellow stripes of course, but then we are different. You are green."

Clara knew that Carl was very proud of his stripes. He had often said that he was sure that when he passed through the chrysalis he would be a really bright colour, judging by his present beauty.

Very soon after that, Carl's body began to harden and change and he became set into his chrysalis shape. Clara looked on this enviously, because she knew that when he emerged Carl would be gone and she would be alone.

She wandered about, munching the flowers and leaves, and one day she found herself by the still water once again. The grasshopper was nowhere near, so she decided to have another good look.

She stared and stared into the water and wondered about the stripes on her back. They did not go straight along her back like Carl's but in a kind of spiral around her, as if she was wrapped up in something of which she could only see the edge.

Then one day Carl's chrysalis began to wriggle and struggle,

and out crawled a damp and bedraggled creature with Carl's face and Carl's eyes but with a large brown wing each side.

The new Carl sat in the sun for a while as Carla watched him and he gradually spread his wings. They were brown with yellow blotches on them each side and he spread them joyously.

"Look at me!" he cried. "Look at how fine my wings are! I have waited so long for this! Now I can fly! I can fly!"

Poor Carla remained there on the ground, watching him fly and wishing that she could join him there in the sky. She was so lonely that she wandered about constantly, but was drawn again and again to the still water. In the glassy mirror of the water she examined the stripes along her back, that were now clear to be seen and maybe a little broader each day.

Then one day she realised that her body was wrapped in a bandage of some kind, seemingly made of thin tissue that was coloured at the edges. She got the occasional glimpse of orange and yellow and a luminescent blue, which surprised her. She wondered how she had come to be wrapped in this stuff, and what would happen if she tried to wriggle out from under it all and see what lay beneath. How could she know what colour she was if she was wrapped up like that?

She became quite angry about all this. She wriggled and struggled with all her might, trying to release herself from the tissue that surrounded her.

While she was struggling the grasshopper came by and watched her. Then he said, "Carla, what are you doing?"

"I am trying to get rid of this stuff that is wrapped all around me."

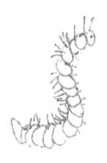 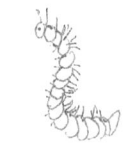

"Why do you want to do that?" asked the grasshopper.

"Because I want to see what colour I am."

"Why do you need to know that?" asked the grasshopper.

"Because I want... all I want in the whole world is to understand why all the other caterpillars in the wood are now flying around happily and I am left here. My body never changes like theirs have and I will never be a butterfly- never!" cried Carla, and she wept bitter tears. She lay there by the still pool in despair.

The grasshopper looked at her with a wise and kindly look. "I think you can fly."

"Don't be silly! Caterpillars can't fly."

"Maybe you are not a caterpillar."

"What do you mean, 'maybe I'm not a caterpillar?' " said Carla, crossly.

"I think the tissue that surrounds you... I think all that stuff is your own wings."

"Wings? I haven't got wings, you stupid grasshopper!" and she crawled away into the wood, angry with the grasshopper; angry with the whole world for leaving her here alone in the wood without any companions and without any hope.

She thought about Carl flying around with his beautiful brown and yellow wings. She realised that he had never come to see her there alone on the ground, but she had stood by him all the time while he waited and longed to be a butterfly so much. She had been his friend, why could he not be her friend?

She sat in the sun, watching the butterflies flying. She wished and wished that she could flap her wings like that. She wished

that the grasshopper had been right, that she had wings, and that if she did this… and that… then she might…

Suddenly she was flying. She was soaring in the air and spinning around. What had happened? Was this a dream? She landed carefully by the still pond and looked down at herself. There, reflected in the pond, were the same eyes, the same face, but behind them the slim and beautiful body of the most beautiful butterfly she had ever seen.

Along her wings - they were her own wings!- were colours of blue and yellow and orange, that made Carl's furry wings look drab.

She had been a butterfly for a long, long time and did not realise it, because Carl's magic mirror had deceived her. But surely she had known, deep down in her body, that she was different from him? She had been through her chrysalis long ago and she was waiting for him to catch her up!

She suddenly felt stupid and foolish but filled with joy, and leaping into the air, she soared upwards and upwards, spreading her wings into the sun.

The Bowl

The process of personal growth requires that you look deep inside yourself, to find out who you truly are...

It was a large earthenware bowl and it had been buried for many years. I had been looking for some time, searching in the ground for signs of where it was buried. Gradually I began to notice the circular shape in the earth. I felt gently round it with my fingers and sure enough there was the rim, jutting out slightly.

It was some time before I was able to distinguish clearly the patterns on the rim. I became afraid that other people may tread upon it, so I marked out a private place around it. Every day, whenever I had a moment, I came to that place to discover more. I saw that there were markings around the rim, which may have been damaged - a few chips here and there, maybe even a slight crack - but otherwise the rim made a perfect circle there, buried in the earth.

I set about digging round the circle and feeling under the bowl with my finger. I was very careful lest I break it in my searching, so I asked a friend to help me. We both worked at it, gradually removing the earth around the bowl, until the shape was clear and the bowl stood there in the hole we had made.

Then it was time to remove the bowl from the earth. We tried to lift it, but it was too heavy! The only thing was to make it lighter, so we set about removing the dirt from the bowl. There was a lot of accumulated rubbish that had collected in the bowl over the years. Some of it was quite unpleasant to see and to handle, but with care and gentleness we removed the dirt, bit by bit, careful not to damage the bowl.

It was almost empty when I said, "Let's take it out of the hole and place it in the sunshine where we can see it more clearly."

So we did that, gently lifting the bowl out onto the soft grass,

THE BOWL

where it stood, dirty and cracked in the morning sun. I took the softest cloth I could find and gently cleaned the bowl until it gleamed in the light and the patterns inside and out began to show clearly. It was a good bowl, large and commodious, and it gleamed. I was proud of it, and it was mine.

I placed it on the shelf in my house. For a long time I admired it and showed it to my friends. They exclaimed with wonder at the hard work it had taken to remove it from the earth and clean it up. But as the days passed I was busy with other things, and gradually over the weeks, the bowl filled up with bits and pieces, until I couldn't see the inside any more.

I wanted to see inside - to run my hands around its curving centre and feel its slightly gritty surface - but it was filled with all my things. So I decided to empty it again, and take out the letters, car keys, old stamps, rubber bands, screws, pins and buttons that had accumulated there.

Why, I wondered, had I worked so hard to empty this bowl and brought it into my house, only to fill it up again with a new collection of things? I polished the bowl and placed it with care on the table and admired it for a long time.

Then my wise friend came to my house and he saw the bowl sitting there. "That bowl is useless," he said.

I did not like him to criticise my beautiful bowl. "It is not!" I cried.

"It is useless because there is nothing in it," he remarked.

I laughed, "Well you should have seen it last week: it was full to the brim with stuff! I had to empty it because I couldn't see the lovely patterns inside it."

"So it was full, and then you emptied it," he mused.

"Now it is very useful!" I realised. "It is not useless - now it is empty I can put things in it again!"

"So it has become useful by being empty?"

"Yes." I stroked the rim of the bowl with my fingers, glad that I had emptied it and was now able to see the patterns inside.

My friend set me a puzzle that day. How could I make my bowl useful at all times and forever? I was sure this was one puzzle I could solve. I went to the well and got some water. I filled the bowl to the brim. Everyone was able to have a drink. When the level in the bowl fell, I was able to fill it up again every day. Surely now my bowl was useful?

But then I was alone in the house for two weeks and the water in the bowl began to stagnate. I was unable to put more water in it unless I poured it all away, washed the bowl and started again. Once more, I had to empty my bowl to make it useful to me! So I left it empty, ready for anyone who wanted to use it.

My friend came again and I said, "I cannot solve this puzzle! How can I make my bowl useful at all times and forever?"

He took up the bowl and silently led me to a small spring, where water trickled out of the rock. He placed the bowl on its side, where the water could trickle in and trickle out again over the rim at the bottom, leaving a small, clear pool of fresh running water in the curve of the bowl.

"Now drink" he said. I drank. The water flowed into and out of my bowl as it lay there under the spring, filled with fresh, clean water, at all times and forever.

The Square Man

Rigid ideas and unreasonable expectations are an important block to personal growth...

Once upon a time, there was a round world, full of round people. The round people bumped against one another but they moved along smoothly and there were no sharp edges. Everyone got along reasonably well. But into the round world came a square man. He had sharp edges. He didn't like the round people, because the round people were different.

"I believe," announced the square man, "that the world should be square. Then I would fit into it perfectly and I wouldn't keep knocking my edges on these round people."

So the square man got together with some other square people, and together they created a little square world in which they could settle together. The trouble was that they interlocked and created a big block of square people. They were completely stuck. They didn't know what to do. The round people were able to move forward and bump into one another without hurting each another. The square people were stuck in one position and they couldn't move any more.

So the square man thought he would ask the Wise Man what he should do.

He said, "Wise Man, what can I do, because I have created a little square world for me to be in with all my square friends, but we don't seem to be able to move or do anything. We are just stuck, what can we do?"

The Wise Man said, "Well, if each of you goes out among the round people, you will find you will be able to move forward and do things."

So the square man went out among the round people. The

round people bumped into him and knocked off his edges, as he twiddled and twirled among them.

Eventually, he went back to the Wise Man and he said, "Well, I've been among the round people for a long time but I am still square. What can I do?"

The Wise Man laughed and said, "Look into the mirror!"

The square man looked into the mirror and saw that he was quite a different shape. All his sharp edges had been knocked off. Although he was not quite perfectly round, he was round enough to fit with all the other round people.

He couldn't go back to his square friends, because he didn't fit there either, so he went on bumping against all the round people, until he too was perfectly round.

The Case

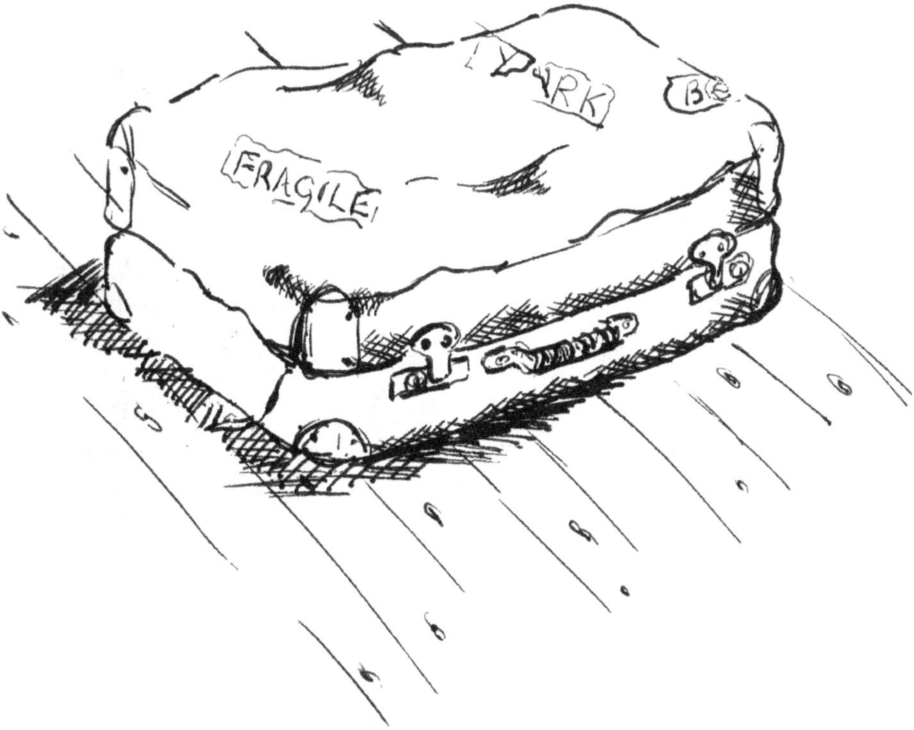

The pain of the past can be a great burden, which must be examined before it can be relinquished...

It was a dark brown, old-fashioned, leather suitcase of indeterminate age, and it was locked. It was given to me by my mother and I carried it about with me all my life. It had labels all over it, of countries far away, trips made by previous generations and far-flung countries with names we don't use any more. I took the suitcase everywhere I went. When I went to school it was there, weighing me down. Later it took up space in the boot of my car - space which may have been better used to store extra books and equipment. It came with me when I moved house. Rather than leave it behind, I threw away precious toys and brought the suitcase instead. I was an adult before I dared to put it down and think about it.

One day I decided to try and find the key. I asked everyone in the family where the key was and they didn't know. I wondered what might be inside. I remembered my mother placing in it, when I was very young, a silver bracelet I had worn as a baby. I wanted to see that and hold it - to see the size of my tiny wrist at that age - but I couldn't open the case and get at it.

Then I spoke to a wise woman who knew about these things. Together we wondered, thought and speculated about what might be the story of the suitcase. First of all we looked at the outside. We examined the labels carefully and tried to work out which grandmother or grandfather had taken which trip, but it did not help me in my quest. I really wanted to know what was inside. Together we wondered what was inside. We speculated and cogitated about the contents of the case.

In my mind's eye there were terrible things inside. I was afraid to open it, lest those things leap out at me and eat me.

THE CASE

Gradually my fears calmed. I realised that the terrible things would be dead now and maybe they had lost their power over me. Then I began to feel deprived and lost, excluded from the secrets of the case. I wanted to hide the case away and stop being obsessed by it, so I angrily threw it away into the cupboard and tried not to think about it for a long time.

As the years passed, I found that I badly needed to know what was in that case. I thought about it every day and did not feel able to live my life fully without the knowledge it contained. So I took it out again and dragged it with me once more to the wise woman.

I raged against the case and the fact that it was locked. The wise woman sat and waited for me to express my rage. I turned my rage upon her and said, "Why are you so indifferent to what is in this case? It is life and death to me! Why are you so dismissive of what is so important to me?"

The wise woman said then, in a quiet, gentle voice, that the suitcase was never mine. It still belonged to my mother. I was shocked by this. Of course the case was mine! It was my gift, the only real gift that my mother, in her inadequacy, ever gave me. I had made it my life's work to carry it about for her. I had surely earned the right for it to be mine! I stormed out of the room, leaving the wise woman alone with the soft smile that enraged me. I shed bitter tears. Alone in my room, I began to tear at the leather, wrench at the lock, but the case would not open. I knew that if I could only open the case - if I tried hard enough - it would open and I would know the secrets of my heart and my mother's heart. I would know WHY.

At last, I went back to the wise woman. I left the case at home. I felt alone without it, lost and vulnerable. I wept for my loneliness; for my wasted years carrying the case, which would never open of itself and reveal my mother to me. For in my mind's eye in the case was my mother, carrying it for her mother. I realised that she had carried it for her mother and maybe my grandmother had carried it in her turn. Each mother within her mother carried the case: it got heavier with each succeeding generation.

Then one day, within my mind's eye, I dared to open the case to see what was inside. It was a terrible black hole that ate everything in its path. I was afraid and closed the case hurriedly. I knew that I would never dare to truly unlock the case, but equally, I would never give it to my child to carry. Surely I should take out the bracelet and give that to my child, and throw the rest away?

So I took the case to the wise woman, and with her help I cut it open. I sliced through the wonderful labels that spoke of past dreams and disillusionment. I reached in with a trembling hand and felt inside. It was filled with hurt, resentment and unrequited love. Now they were released, the case was overflowing with feelings, fears and memories of past dreams. There in the midst of it all lay my silver bracelet - not shining, as I had imagined it, but drab and tarnished. The curling, faded photos; the little unspoken thoughts and un-given gifts; the unrealised dreams and terrible shame - I knew nothing of. They were not mine. Clutching the bracelet (the only thing that was truly mine) I turned and walked away.

The Coat

When ordinary kindness and concern for others becomes compulsive, a major block to personal growth has been created...

It was a large, warm coat that wrapped me in its folds, within which I felt safe. It was given to me by my mother, who said nothing about it to me at the time, but I came to understand that it would keep me warm against the cold winds that often blew, so I wore it always. There were pockets on the outside, and secret pockets in the inside. In fact there were so many pockets, I sometimes couldn't find what I wanted, unless I searched very hard and for a long time.

In the beginning it was smooth and soft. It blew in the wind and fresh air wafted around me within the folds. I soon found the pockets useful. They were large and there was room for all kinds of treasures in them. I went about collecting treasures and hid them in my pockets until they were all filled. People saw me in the coat and said, "Look how she is growing!" I stood tall and proud of being big, but in my secret heart I knew that I was much smaller than my coat.

When I wanted a comb, there was a comb in my pocket, ready for use. When I wanted some bread, sure enough, there was bread. It was good to know that I was never in want, that everything I wanted was there, in my coat.

Then I saw some small thin people who did not have a big coat like mine, so I gave them some of the bread out of my pocket to help them grow strong.

It made them happy and I knew that they would never be hungry if they always had bread in their secret pocket, so I taught them how to find bread for themselves.

"You can have everything you want, just when you need it!" I told them. "Just make sure that you keep some ready in your

THE COAT

coat, and you will never be hungry again!"

I gathered up more bread and put it in my pockets and so did one of the small, thin people. There would be some for us and some for the all other people who may need it. My coat grew larger and larger, and heavier and heavier. Soon my little thin friend didn't look quite so small and the wind didn't blow around my legs any more. I felt stifled and hot but I needed my coat.

Sometimes I tried taking my coat off, just to feel cool, but I found I couldn't manage for long without it, for I felt very vulnerable to the cold winds that might blow.

Again and again, I took my coat off and gradually began to like the lightness and freshness of being without it. Yet I always put it on again when the wind blew a little cool.

I wondered why I wore such a heavy big coat and other people didn't. So I asked a girl who was quite small, but not tiny. She carried a coat on her arm but didn't seem to have to wear it, unless it was really cold.

"Why do you not wear a coat?" I asked.

"I have one ready for the winter," she replied, "but I don't need to wear it today. Today it is not cold. Why are you wearing yours?"

"I always wear it." I replied. "It is useful, because there are big pockets, and I can always have what I want straight away and so can anyone else who needs it."

I offered her some bread, but she refused, saying she wasn't hungry. I suggested that she put the bread in the pocket of the coat that lay over her arm, in case she was hungry later, but

she refused again, saying she could always get some later if she needed it. I felt so sad that this girl, who was thinner than me, should not take some of my bread. I found myself thinking about her all day long, wondering if she was hungry. I wondering if I ought to go and find her and make sure she hadn't changed her mind. The next day I met a large strong man. He was very tall and he wore no coat.

"Why do you not wear a coat?" I asked.

"I don't need one," he said. "If I get cold I move about and do things, and I'm soon warm."

"What do you do without pockets?" I asked.

"I don't need pockets!" he cried. "I know where I can get what I need. Why should I carry a lot of stuff about with me that I don't need?"

"What if you find someone who is hungry?" I asked.

"It is better if you teach them how to make their own bread, for then they can be fed for life. If you give them your bread, they will just come back for more, next time they are hungry. Why should you fetch bread and carry it for them to eat?"

I felt hurt and misjudged by this. "It's better than nothing." I replied.

"But better still is fresh, good bread," the strong man said. "Why don't you teach them how to make their own bread?"

"But I don't know how." I said. I knew then that I didn't know how to make my own bread and had always relied on what I could pick up and that no one else wanted.

He looked at me and asked, "What have you got in your pockets?"

THE COAT

I was so glad to have the chance to tell him. "Everything!" I cried. I pulled out of my pockets all the treasures I had collected. I proudly laid them out on the ground.

It took a long time but when all the pockets were empty, I could see how much I had collected over the years. Then I looked carefully at what was there and did not feel quite so proud. How dirty some of the things now were! How stale and useless the bread was!

I wondered if the strong man thought me rather small and insignificant without my coat. At least with my coat on I was easily seen in a crowd and everyone knew I was there.

He looked at me without the big pockets and said, "Now I can see the real you under all that stuff."

I felt strange, but it was good to know that the real me under the coat was at least visible, and it would seem from his reaction that I was acceptable, even though I was a lot smaller than I first might have appeared.

As I stood there in the gentle breeze, I felt the air stir around my legs. I noticed how my coat was distorted by the pockets that had been stretched out of shape by having too much stuffed into them.

I felt again the initial lightness and the soft feel of the coat around me, and thought about the day I had first received it from my mother. I wondered why she had told me to wear it always.

Surely she had known how heavy it would become in the heat? Surely she could have guessed what I would do with so many pockets? I became very angry and decided to ask her why she had burdened me in this way. I went to her bed, where she lay dying. I wore the coat but the pockets were empty. Seeing her so small and thin there on the bed, I asked her, "Mother, why did you give me this coat?"

She held the soft folds of the garment for a moment as if she were remembering something very special. "I gave you this because it was the only way I knew how to keep you warm," she said. "I knew no other way, because my mother gave me a coat like this to wear when I was a child, and I wore it always in obedience to her will. It was hard and I always wondered what it may have been like if I had taken the coat off when I grew older, but I never dared to do it."

All at once I knew that I could take off my coat, for there was another way to keep warm. "Would you mind if I took the coat off now?" I asked my mother.

"If you can be safe and warm without it, of course you can," she said and she smiled at me a loving, warm smile.

I took the coat off and placed it around my mother's ageing shoulders. "This will keep you warm, I don't need it now."

"What if the winter wind starts to blow?" she asked me anxiously.

"Then I shall weave myself a blanket to wrap myself in for the winter. I will make it out of all the wisdom you gave me."

"And what about pockets? Won't you need them?"

"I will go and find my small thin friend. Together we will ask the strong man to teach us how to make bread."

Leaving my mother snug and warm in her bed asleep at last, I set off to find my friend. I felt the warm wind upon me as I walked.

The Dance

Spiritual growth is facilitated by close, trusting relationships....

I woke up to find myself in a dark and swirling place where dancing figures brushed me as they passed.

"Stay!" I cried. "Stay and tell me where I am!" But the dancing figures danced on and ignored me.

I lay in that place of darkness waiting for someone to touch me. At last they touched me and I cried out: "Stay! Tell me who I am!" But they ignored me and danced on.

Again something touched me and I reacted saying: "Stop! Stay with me because I don't know what I must do."

The dancing figure wrapped itself around me for a while but did not answer. I learned to wrestle myself free and move about alone.

So I lay in the dark wondering where I was and who I was. What I must do? But no one came and no one cared. I was alone.

The dancing figures were my friends. They knew what to do. They danced, so I danced. They were still and so I was still.

We danced together in a primitive rhythm. My body grew in strength and in the rhythm was the dance. I was a dancer and became the dance; I knew how to dance and I loved the dance! I loved to feel them brush me gently as they passed.

How I loved to make my own circles in my little dark world, knowing they were there with me! Then as I grew, I could not feel them any more. But I had learned how to dance like them in the dark, so I forgot them and danced on until there was no more room to dance.

But then it was time to pass into the light and the dancers were gone into a dream. In the light of day there were no soft touches

on my arms. Instead, there were strong, enclosing embraces that held me tightly and did not let me go. I wrestled myself free so I could be the dance once again.

The dance faded from my mind until it was no more than a fleeting shadow that touched my eye corner in the fragment of an idea. I was alone with a sense of something missing, but I knew how to dance.

I looked into myself, searching for that vague memory of the other dancers, but they eluded me. For many years I stared into the mirror, searching my face for the answer to the mystery of who I was and who would want to dance with me.

Voices often came to me in that bright world, calling me and asking me questions about things I did not know, so I didn't answer because I could not. I was dancing in a forgotten dream and there I stayed.

Then someone touched me lightly on the arm. I remembered my dancers and was glad. So I closed my eyes and danced the silent dance. But she did not know how to dance with me.

She did not brush gently past and pass on, like the dancers in my dream. She kept holding on to me so tightly that I had to wrestle myself away, for I was dreaming of a touch that does not hold.

She told me I was bad because I did not know how to hold her and dance in her new way. I was hurt and angry because this was not my dance; I danced alone. It was good and I knew it with all my heart. It was her dance that was different from mine!

I tried to dance her dance but I always stumbled and got it all wrong. She left me alone to make my lonely circles. All was right again until she begged me again and again to hold her.

I was happy if I did not listen and kept my eyes closed and danced alone, but when I opened my eyes there were always people telling me that my dance was wrong. They railed and shouted at me. They harangued me about the way I danced and said I was bad because I danced alone. I did not understand. They did not know that I am the dance.

Then one day I explained to my friend that I dance alone and the dance is me, and she understood.

"Teach me to dance alone, like you," she said.

So we made a new dance. I stood a good way off and danced alone and she mirrored everything I did. I danced alone and so did she. We danced alone together. As she danced my dance, I saw my dance in her body. We danced in unison for many days and it was good.

"Now try this," she said. She stepped towards me. I stepped forward and we danced on. "Now a little nearer. I won't hurt you or trap you," she said and she laid her hand gently on mine. We danced on with hands touching. Her body moved with mine.

Her hand lay on my hand with such love that I let it lie there, trusting her to let me go whenever I needed to dance free and alone. We danced our new dance. Her touch was loving and good and I knew that I could break away and be free.

She smiled at me with kindness and said: "This is the best dance in the world." Once again I could live my dream and be the dance and the dancer.

This is how we made our new dance together in the clear light of day.

The Jewel

Spiritual growth is blocked by a thirst for personal power...

In a small town a long way away from here, there lived a chicken farmer with a secret. Every day he went to look after his chickens. He counted how many eggs had been laid and how many little chicks had hatched out of the eggs. When he saw the little yellow chicks he was pleased, because he knew they would grow into strong, healthy chickens and one day they would lay eggs for him.

Sometimes he took some eggs and chickens to the market, for if he did not, he would have far too many. He loved to walk around his farm and observe the chicks and chickens stepping and pecking around him. He loved his chickens, but he was reluctant to send any of them away. He knew in his secret heart that one day one of the eggs would hatch and inside there would be a jewel of great price. This jewel would make him the most powerful man in the world.

So every time an egg was laid, he carefully scrutinised it, trying to guess what was inside. Every time he went to market he worried that he had given away the jewel, and so he found all kinds of secret ways of making sure that the jewel was not in any of the eggs he sold.

Many years went by and he never saw a jewel hatch out of any egg. He began to say to himself that really it didn't matter if he didn't have the jewel; he was happy with his chickens and his eggs; happy with his pretty house on the hillside where he could walk alone and undisturbed with his chickens all around him.

Then one day he woke up and knew at once that the jewel was there on the farm. He rushed out to the chicken house and

searched everywhere for a long time. He took the eggs that had been laid, placed them in an incubator and watched them carefully for many days.

One by one, the eggs hatched. A bedraggled baby chick fell out of each broken shell, drying quickly in the warmth, until chick got up on its wobbly legs and began to walk around, its fluffy feathers turning a delicate shade of yellow as he watched. He loved to see the tiny baby chicks in their fresh new innocence. His heart warmed to them but he watched the remaining eggs until there was one last egg left. He waited and waited but the egg wouldn't hatch.

He decided to break the egg, even though he knew that, if there were a tiny chick inside, this would kill it. He wanted the jewel so much that he was prepared to sacrifice just one precious tiny chicken, if needs be.

So he took a hammer and broke the egg. All over the table there was the sticky albumen and the yellow yolk. There was no chick, but somewhere amongst the mess was a tiny, shiny object. He took it in his fingers, disappointed that it was so small.

He washed it and examined it under a magnifying glass. It was a very beautiful jewel, something like a diamond, only it was so perfect, with facets so clear and reflective, that it broke the sunlight into a hundred separate colours.

He looked and looked at the jewel, almost losing himself in the magical world of light and colour that was played out before him. He looked and looked, while his chickens went hungry and the sun set. The baby chickens huddled against the fence in the pouring rain.

He looked and dreamed and wondered while many days passed. His baby chickens died and the adult chickens wandered away. Then he looked around him and saw his farm in ruins, but in his hands there was the precious jewel he had waited for all his life. What need had he of his farm now? He was the most powerful man in the world!

So he set off into the town to seek his fortune, armed with the jewel, that he kept secret in his pocket. He must not let anyone see it or they would want it or steal it from him. With his new-found power, he set himself up in the town as the mayor and brought about several important reforms.

People came to him with wonderful gifts, which he gladly received. There were clothes, a wonderful house, a grand piano - which he didn't know how to play, but it looked good in his lounge so he didn't care.

Beautiful women came to him. One of them, called Julina, wanted to marry him, so he married her. He was rich and no longer lonely but he still had the secret jewel. It worried him that he might lose it.

So one night he stroked Julina's hair and he said, "Julina, I have a secret. Promise me that you will never tell anyone about it, if you love me."

"Of course I love you," Julina said. "Tell me your secret."

"I have a magical jewel," he said, "which has made me the most powerful man in the world. I am afraid that if anyone knew, they would steal it from me."

Julina was of course at once very interested. "Darling," she said. "Show it to me."

THE JEWEL

He took the jewel out of the secret pocket where he kept it, and showed it to her.

"It's rather small," she said. He remembered that this had been his first thought too.

"Yes, but I can do so much with it!" he cried. "I certainly wouldn't have got here without it. I wouldn't have you," he said, smiling at her, "or this," he said, waving his hand at the luxurious bed with magnificent drapes.

Julina was examining the jewel, staring and staring at it, lost in its beauty. He looked at her looking at it and thought that she had never been more beautiful.

For many days she stared and stared. She grew more beautiful in his eyes until he loved her more than he had ever loved anyone or anything. One day she looked away from the jewel for a moment and looked at him. Her eyes were shining with power.

He knew then what he wanted to do. "Julina," he said, "I want you to have the jewel."

Smiling, she took the jewel and she became the most powerful woman in the world. He loved her but her power took her away from him. She travelled the world and soon ignored him.

So he went up the hillside and began to rebuild his chicken farm. He sold the eggs and chickens at a good price and soon he had made a comfortable home for himself.

Julina came to visit him but her eyes were filled with dreams and she didn't see him. He felt sad and lonely but he knew that the woman he loved had what she wanted. That made him happy.

Then one day, a poor bedraggled creature came up the hill through the rain. He knew at once that it was Julina. He came out to meet her. He gave her his coat and brought her into the warmth by the fire. As she warmed up, she told her story. She had lost the jewel and all her power had been stripped from her. She had lost everything that the jewel had given her.

So he folded her in his arms and held her tight. He knew that he loved her more, as her tears dried by the light of the small candle, than he had ever loved her before.

They lived on the hillside together for the rest of their days. The chickens laid their eggs and the yellow fluffy chicks hatched out. Hand in hand, they walked in the sunshine as the chickens stepped and pecked around them.

Ivy Tree

Spiritual growth includes a movement through pain towards greater wisdom....

The tree stood by a river that flowed slowly through the scattered woodland. It was a small tree, with blossom in the spring and dark, red fruit in the autumn.

Round the trunk ivy grew, with dark green leaves unfurling and tendrils spreading as the seasons progressed. The ivy grew quickly but the tree grew faster. The ivy spread slowly up the trunk and along the branches, but the twigs of the tree unfurled their tiny green leaves each spring, and in summer the dense, leafy branches left the ivy in shade.

The ivy said to the tree, "I need you to hold me up and enable me to grow tall. I need to find the rough places in your bark for my suckers to grip you tightly to keep me from falling. I will drink the rain as it pours and dribbles along your branches and down your trunk. My roots are intertwined with yours. We share the same earth, you and I."

The tree said to the ivy, "I need you to wrap yourself around me, to protect me from the strong winds in winter, to make me strong and enlarge the girth of my trunk with your woody stems. With you around me I will look stronger. I will seem to be fresh and green, even in the winter snows. I know that we are friends, that we share the same space, see the same sky and know the soft kisses of the rain as it falls upon us."

Years passed. When winter came, the leaves fell off the tree and only the ivy leaves remained. They were dark and shining, and the tendrils waved and twisted around the bare branches as the ivy grew higher still, reaching for the sun.

When summer came and the tree woke up again, the tiny

leaves unfurled but there was less and less of the little tree visible to passers by. Soon the tree seemed to consist only of ivy, in the vague shape of a tree, dark against grey skies and rustling in the winter wind.

The ivy said to the tree, "See! I am greater than you are! I am greener and stronger and I can reach all the hidden parts of you. You are overcome. You are my slave! I have conquered you!"

The soft voice of the tree, hidden within the ivy, whispered, "You are choking me! The life is going out of me! I cannot reach the light so that I can feed and grow. I do not wish to be your slave! I will not let you conquer me!"

So the little tree grew as wide as it could, trying to burst out of the ivy stems, but the stems were fixed fast to the trunk and would not budge. The little tree grew taller than ever, reaching higher and higher into the sky, searching for light and space. The trunk grew thinner and thinner and was barely able to sustain this new growth, but the thick stems of the ivy stood fast.

The tree cried out in triumph, "See! I am taller than you are and the strength you have given me is helping me to stand tall! I will spread my roots wider, and reach higher and higher until you cannot reach me!"

The ivy said nothing for a long time.

The tree spoke once more, "I never wanted you to be clutching me like this: if you had left me alone I would be a beautiful tree, able to grow into my own shape. Now I have been shaped by you and I hate you for that!"

Again, the ivy said nothing and was still and quiet.

Then the tree grew angry and said, "I wish that the forester would come and slice your stems above the roots, so I could breathe and grow to any shape I chose!"

The tree listened but there was no sound, only the soft whisper of falling ivy leaves. Slowly the leaves fell to the ground and the ivy was silent and still.

The tree came to realise that the ivy had died. All through the winter, both tree and ivy stood entwined, mute and still, as if both ivy and tree were dead.

But spring came and the tree put out the tiny buds and little twigs grew from among the woody dead stems of the ivy. Blossom formed, white and pure, in a celebration of new life.

When the wind blew a little, the blossom fell. The tree wept for the ivy, which still wound itself in death around the tree.

The ivy was silent and still but the dead stems were strong and woody, giving strength to the trunk of the tree, which was barely visible within.

As the seasons passed, the tree stood tall and alone in the forest by the stream, which flowed silently by.

The Man with No Name

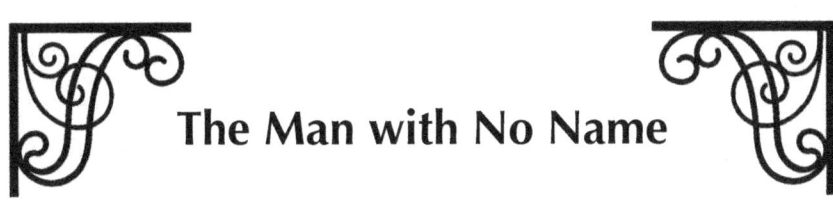

The path to personal growth is a search for the authentic self...

Once upon a time when the world was very new and I did not know my name, I was playing "Follow my Leader" along the road. If the Leader turned left, then I turned left. It was good fun because I had nothing to worry about. I knew that as long as I followed the Leader exactly, everything would work out fine and we would all find our way home.

Then when I got bigger I was able to find my way home all by myself, because I remembered which way the Leader went and I went that way every time. But a feeling grew inside me that I wanted to try new roads.

I asked the Leader about that and he taught me the Rules. "If you turn right, that is the wrong way and you will get covered with yellow shame dust. If you turn left that is the right way and you will stay clean."

So I went along the road alone and did what I was told. I always turned left. Very soon I was back where I started. I thought about that for a long time and decided to turn right and see what happened to me. I turned right and went a little way along the road but I was worried and came back very soon.

I told the Leader, "I turned right and the road looked exactly the same kind of road as the other way but this time it seemed to be going somewhere exciting and different; tell me: why is that the wrong way to go?"

The Leader became angry with me because I had broken the Rule. He showered me with yellow shame dust because I had questioned his authority. I was ignored by the others because I was bright yellow with shame dust. I was told I must never break the Rule again.

So I spent my days walking in circles with all the others. I was told that if I said I was sorry for breaking the Rule, then I would be clean again. I said sorry and I was washed clean again. The Leader was very pleased with my walking in circles and praised me for being so obedient to the Rule. But secretly I became so bored with the circle road! I wanted so much to explore and examine all the other byways!

Eventually I knew I must leave the circle road if I was going to live my life to the full. I did not care about the shame dust. I became angry with the Leader, because a good Leader ought to think more about people and their need to explore.

"I hate the Leader!" I said. "I will do what I think is right! If I am mistaken then so be it. It's my life. I will go to the right. I will." And I did.

"Come back!" shouted the Leader. "You have broken the Rule and the punishment is to be ignored and have no name and no identity."

They dragged me back and threw me into a vat of shame dust. They made me walk the circle road alone. I had no name and no identity. I was very angry with the people for treating me this way. I had only tried to explore a bit of the world. It's such a wonderful world, with so much to see and do!

I hated them all. I plotted and planned for the day when I would be free. I knew that the Rule was stupid and I only wanted to explore. I knew that asking for forgiveness would remove the

yellow dust, but I could not apologise when there had been no wrong-doing. So I stayed yellow.

Then one day when the trees on the right of the road were covered in spring green; when the hills were beckoning me to come to them and I could hear the call of the birds, I turned my steps to the right. I ran and ran until I could no longer hear the people calling me.

I had no name and no identity but I had my freedom.

It was a straight road and a good one. It seemed to be going somewhere. As I walked I decided on a name for myself: "Yellow Walker." I sang a little and decided on an identity: I am The Yellow Person who Walks Straight. Life was good: at last I had a path, an identity and a name.

Then I came to a place where there were other yellow walkers. They walked straight, just like me, and I joined them.

"I am Yellow Walker," I said. They seemed to find that acceptable.

"I am the Person Who Walks Straight," I said to another walker.

So am I," came the reply, as if that was the usual way to be.

I was among friends! We walked side by side for some time. I forgot about how yellow I was. Then one day a path opened up to the left, with a wonderful stream beside it and kingfishers darting. I turned to explore this wonderful path.

"We must all walk straight!" they all cried. "We must not turn left! We must walk straight!" They dragged me back onto

the straight road.

"We have a Rule," said the Leader. "We must always walk straight and turn neither to the right nor to the left. We must look straight ahead and never stray from the path. That is the right way. For your punishment, you will be washed clean of every trace of yellow. You will be ignored."

I was washed clean of all the yellow and no one spoke to me. I walked on. Here was another set of Rules but, as before, I badly needed to break them!

One evening when the dusk was falling, I set off quietly down a little path to the right where a little waterfall trickled over the rocks and butterflies darted among the flowers. It was enchanting and wonderful. I was enjoying the walk when suddenly there was a hand on my shoulder.

"I am a policemen," said a voice. "You are a criminal, because you are not yellow and also you have broken a Rule. You will lose your name and your identity and you will go to prison."

So they threw me into prison and I was no longer Yellow Walker. I had lost my name and my identity.

I languished in prison for some time and became very angry indeed, because all I had ever wanted to do with my life was explore the beautiful world. The stupid Rules didn't allow this.

While I was in prison I had plenty of time to think. I thought: "I am a prisoner because I choose freedom. Therefore my new name is Freedom Chooser. I am a prisoner because I love to explore new byways and see all the beauty of the world. Therefore my new identity will be The One Who Loves The World."

Soon it was time to be set free and I walked out. I spoke to my jailers and said, "You can keep me in prison; you can take away my name and my identity, but now I know my own name and my own identity. No one can take that away from me."

"I am Freedom Chooser," I said. "I am the One Who Loves The World."

Sam's Garden

The path of spiritual growth can be blocked entirely by addiction and compulsive behaviour.......

Sam lived in a little house that was small, but all his own. Every day the sun shone in at the window, but the glass was so dusty he could hardly see. He didn't care, because as long as he had his fiddle he could play until his heart raced with pleasure and longing, for something he couldn't quite understand.

Sam woke up one day and saw that his garden was unkempt. "I have neglected my garden. I really should do something about it," he said. He went out into the garden and he saw the bindweed and the lawn rough and un-mown.

He asked his father to help him but he would not. "My son, when you were young I tried to tell you how to make your garden grow but you did not listen. You must do this yourself. I can lend you some tools if you like."

So Sam went home that day with a spade and hoe. Sam pulled at the bindweed until great swathes of it lay on the ground beside him. He cut and pruned and hacked until the garden was piled high with rubbish.

"Now the place looks even worse!" he cried. "How can I get rid of this rubbish?"

His neighbour Dick called over the wall. "Let's have a bonfire!" shouted Dick.

In a trice the weeds and twigs and brambles were burning and smoking and sparks were blowing high into the sky. Sam took out his fiddle and played until the mess in the garden was forgotten.

Weeks went by and the garden was just as he had left it. The spade and the hoe were left out in the rain. Already rusty, they rusted still more.

SAM'S GARDEN

A certain tune began to hum inside his head. It lay at the side of his mind just out of reach. He paced the floor and wondered what the tune was, what it meant, but it would not come to him. He played his fiddle until the strings broke and he could play no longer.

He took his fiddle to be mended by a wise old man. "This fiddle has been used too much," the old man said. "You must not play it so much or it will become unplayable."

The thought of not playing frightened him. When he didn't play, the days were long and lonely and there was no happiness for him. Only when he took up his fiddle did he feel eternal joy, but still there was that elusive tune in his head.

Months went by. Sam was filled with regret that he had failed to look after his garden. Even the fiddle did not fill him with pleasure any more but when it was mended he kept on playing, to forget the wonderful tune he longed to be able to hear.

Eventually he hired a gardener. The garden was cleared and although it looked bare it was tidier. Now Sam could look out of the window and think about the flowers he would plant in the spring.

The gardener had to leave but Sam knew he could do it; the worst of the work was done and he could manage it alone now. But the weeds grew so high he could not clear them as fast as they could grow.

Eventually he sat inside the house and dreamed and felt the shame of the wasted years. He was alone.

Then one day the Wise Man who mended his fiddle said, "I know a friend with a wonderful pond of sweet water that is as

still as glass and deeper than anyone can imagine. He says that when you can see yourself in the sweet water, you will be given your heart's desire."

Sam went to look into the pond, but he saw nothing in it but brown, stagnant water. The kind friend looked at Sam with eyes that knew him and cared for him.

All at once, Sam realised that he had always been alone but now his kind friend was with him. Sometimes he had the strength to go out into the garden.

He saw clearly for the first time how it was laid out, with flowerbeds and vegetable plots and a sweeping wide lawn. Week by week, he described the garden to his kind friend, but there was no advice.

Sam grew angry. "Why won't you help me?" he cried.

"What do you want?" The quiet voice asked.

Want? To hear the music at last, to see the sunshine, know eternal joy... but he couldn't say all this, because this man didn't know about the music. Not yet.

Sam answered, "I want to grow Roses." What? He had never been interested in roses! *Why on earth did he say that?*

So Sam grew roses. He cleared the garden and learned that weeds could be food for the roses, if he made a compost heap. He piled up the weeds and they rotted away, giving out a rich, earthy smell. With the twigs and branches, Sam made a big bonfire. The smoke curled upwards as he said his good-byes to the old garden. All he hoped for, all he lived for now, were the roses. His fiddle was forgotten, because he went out into the garden each day.

SAM'S GARDEN

He held a party to celebrate when the first white rose opened its tiny bud to the sun. The sun shone, people laughed and his secret yearning for the elusive tune was forgotten.

After the party, everyone left. Sam was alone, staring at his precious rose bud. Then he began to feel sadness so deep, it filled Sam until his body was saturated with it. Gradually, as the dawn began to break, there was a whisper of something new in the sadness. There was a fragment of a tune that felt strange, and yet familiar.

Sam lay in his bed filled with a dull ache of sadness, yet with a strange relief, as if he had passed through a place that he would not have to visit again.

He went to see the kind friend, and told him about the rose opening and the sadness. He wept silently there by the still water of the pond while the kind friend waited.

At last, Sam was able to speak what was in his heart. It made him feel shaky and uncertain, but as the words came, one by one, he knew what he wanted. "How can I hear the music?" said Sam.

"Have you tried listening for it?" asked the kind friend. "Let's listen and see if we can hear it."

There by the pool, in a silence that didn't feel so lonely because the friend was there with him, Sam was at last able to hear fragments of the tune that was familiar and yet so new it was fresh and uplifting but it would not stay.

Sam had learned to listen for it in the silent place inside himself. He had learned how to hear his heart's desire. He put his fiddle away in its box and went out into the garden. He spread

compost on the roses. As more blooms opened, he invited people in to see them.

Yet even when people were there in his lovely garden, he longed for quiet and silence. He was gradually discovering more and more of the wonderful tune that brought joy with it. It came slowly and gradually into his heart. He knew now, and had always known, that this was the symphony of himself.

One day Sam was able to take up his fiddle and play his secret symphony. It was beautiful. Children came to hear him. He was able to feel joy at last - a joy he had created for himself.

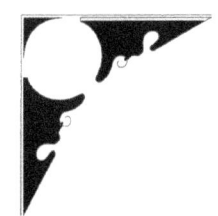 

The Store

An exaggerated sense of responsibility for others can delay progress indefinitely......

My secret storeroom was full of old and dusty things. Some of them had once been very valuable indeed, while others were just junk. It was so crowded in there that it was hard to see which was which. The room was small, dimly lit and musty. For as long as I could remember, it had been my job to look after it.

I knew what the others would say to me if they knew about my secret store: "This store is messy! You have not been minding it properly. You must sort it all out so that you can throw out all the junk!"

I did not want to be ashamed of it if anyone saw inside, so I set about cleaning the store - sorting it all, cleaning out the boxes and ordering all the items. There was a lot to check, but gradually I got a sense of what was there. I even created my own filing system. I kept changing the system as I discovered more and more items. For a small room, it contained a lot. The others never asked me what I was doing. They just went on playing out in the sun while I was busy organising the store.

After many months of ordering and sorting I became impatient to get it done. So I decided to spend all day, every day in the store. I foolishly believed that if I managed to sort it out, then I would be free of my obligation and would be able at last to play outside in the sun. Day and night I worked, sorting and ordering and creating several new filing systems each day.

I tried to tell the others how I was doing but they didn't understand the complex filing system I had created. They obviously didn't want to know. So I remained alone in the store, working and working.

Then I became exhausted and I was ill in bed. Still I worked, planning new filing systems in my head, dreaming of the day when I would be free to go out in the sun like the others did. As I lay in bed, I learned the pleasure of just doing nothing. I listened to the others playing in the sun and wished I had the energy to be out there with them, but I was so exhausted from running the store that I did not have the energy to play. If I did go out, I was only able to watch from the sidelines while the others played. Anyway, I didn't understand the rules of the game because I had never played that way before.

As I learned to sit and do nothing, some new ideas came to me in the blessed silence that fell. I wondered how the others kept their stores in order so well that they had time to play. I watched and listened and learned; I wondered and speculated and dreamed. I became weary of that too, because I had tried so hard to work it all out. Still I had failed to mind my store efficiently enough so that I had time to play with the others.

I lay there in my bed, exhausted. One day I simply gave up in despair. I could not manage this. It was beyond me.

"Someone else can do it!" I cried. At once I realised that I had never been given the job of minding the store but had just decided myself to take the job on.

Who would mind the store if I stopped looking after it? What would happen to all the precious things? Would they be lost forever?

I dreamed as I lay there. In the dream I went to the store and looked at it with one long, loving look. I closed the door and stepped out in the sunshine to play with the others. As I stepped away I knew that there was someone there behind me who had entered by the same door. They had stepped into my shoes but I didn't look back because I didn't want to know who it was.

I slept a long sleep, while in my dreams someone else minded the store. When I awoke, I felt refreshed, for I knew what to do. I got out of my bed and decided not to mind the store that day. It was hard, because I still wanted to put some of my plans into action. However, I found the courage to turn away. It wasn't so difficult then, going out to play.

The others welcomed me and taught me the rules. All the time, I was learning to believe that everything was OK; that there would always be someone minding the store, and it did not have to be me.

But then I realised that I had left my own precious things behind in the store! Who would mind my stuff? Could I go back to the store and just mind my own stuff and leave others to mind theirs? I didn't even know which stuff was mine and which stuff belonged to the others.

I felt ashamed of myself that I should neglect my own precious things, while I worked out all those fancy filing systems to handle everyone else's stuff. I had imagined I had the power to tidy up the whole place, and I had enjoyed being in charge. I had been showing off how clever I was, when all the time I was not minding that part of the store where my own things lay.

Humbly, I went back to reclaim my own things. I carried them with me as I walked, knowing that there was always someone else to mind the store.

The Sailor

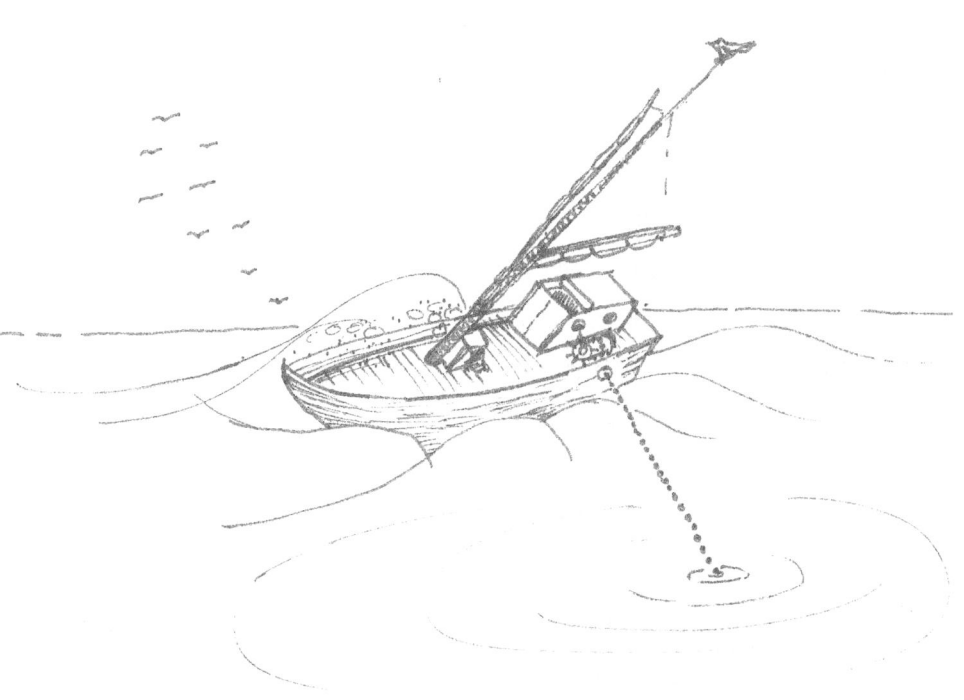

Clinging onto anything that will provide a sense of security, will delay your progress...

There was a man who lived aboard a boat. It was just a little boat in the middle of the ocean but it was built of strong timbers and it had a commodious cabin.

The boat was anchored with a chain a mile long, for the ocean was a mile deep.

The sailor could feel the tug of the anchor when the wind blew strongly as he lay in his warm and cosy cabin. It made him feel safe.

For many years the man remained in the cabin, for he had no need of telescope or sextant. The helm was fixed to move forward and the sails were down, so that he had nothing to do. The anchor held him fast and he could relax in safety.

But one day he heard the call of the wind and the gulls from the other side of the hatch above his head. The call became more and more insistent, until he decided to open the hatch just a little and see what was going on.

He arose from his bunk and reached out. He opened the hatch just a crack and a sweet smell of sea air came to him. He realised how stuffy and stale the air had become in the cabin, because it was a long time since he had opened the hatch. So he breathed in the sweet air and felt the wind in his hair. For a brief moment he tasted freedom.

Every day after that, he opened the hatch a little more, until it was open all day - unless the rain came splashing down, for then he remained inside, safe and warm and protected. It was a good life, but he had tasted freedom.

The taste grew bitter when it rained, for he was trapped inside the cabin. The walls were restricting and there was little space for movement. He was not able easily to stand upright.

One day he noticed that there were oilskins in the corner of the cabin. They were hardly used. So he dressed himself carefully in the oilskins and opened the hatch. The rain came down into the cabin through the opening, so he quickly climbed up onto the deck and closed the hatch behind him.

The wind blew in his face and the rain was in his eyes and he could not see clearly. He was afraid that he may fall over board, so he climbed back into the cabin again.

From this day onward, it was no longer a smooth ride. The boat twitched and strained against the anchor, like a terrier at its leash. The boat was restless but the anchor held her safe. There was always movement. The boat rocked from left to right, left to right, up and over and around and down.

Sometimes the boat seemed to move rapidly forward, but the anchor brought it up short. The boat was jerked back and resumed her normal sideways swing.

Once in a while, a huge wave steamed in and sideswiped the boat. When that happened, the sailor held on tight and hoped for it soon to be over.

But then the Anchor Man arrived and brought with him a parachute anchor.

"What is this?" asked the sailor.

"This anchor will keep you facing the wind," said the Anchor Man. "Then you will not be tossed about so much. If you want to use it, you must wait for a calm day and wind in the anchor that fixes you on the sea floor."

The sailor was afraid. "But then I will not be safe any more!"

"Facing the waves is safest," said the Anchor Man calmly. "Boats are designed to take waves on the bow - not from the beam. This way, your boat will survive the storms that must come."

Leaving the parachute anchor on the deck, the Anchor Man left him alone in the middle of the sea.

The sailor had to decide: would he dare to wind up the fixed anchor and use the parachute anchor instead? He waited until the calmest day, when there was no wind at all and the sea was glassy calm.

He dropped the parachute anchor into the water and watched as it disappeared into the depths. As he watched he saw the deep, invisible currents of water fill the parachute, and the new anchor line gradually grew taught.

Once he knew that the new anchor was working, he gradually wound in the old, heavy anchor chain until the anchor, which had held him safe for so long, lay on the deck, heavy with barnacles and seaweed.

He was not certain that the new parachute anchor would hold him, so he remained watchful. He waited for the next storm. Sure enough, when the boat faced the oncoming waves, things were steadier and the boat felt stronger.

Then the sailor realised something extraordinary. The boat was now steady where before it had been restless - always on the move.

Then he laughed aloud as the truth dawned in his mind. For his whole life he had been swinging at anchor in a broad circle, round and round!

The wind in his hair and the sun on his face was so sweet and exhilarating that he spent more and more time on deck.

Then he found a sextant and telescope in an old box that had always been on the boat but he had never opened it before. The sextant showed him where he was and the telescope revealed misty shores, far away. His heart burst with longing and he yearned to explore.

Day by day, he grew more certain that he must begin to move. So he tripped the parachute anchor. It collapsed and he drew it easily onto the deck. It was less of a burden to lift than the sea floor anchor he had used all his life, until recently. He felt strong and happy.

He waited to see what would happen. The wind blew and he soon realised that he was drifting. He had no idea were he was going. He would soon be completely lost. But then in that moment he realised, he had always been lost. A great surge of energy rose in him. It was time to take charge.

He opened the sail box where the sails had lain for so long. Slowly - because he was not sure how to do it - he worked out how to raise the sails. He pulled and pulled on the ropes and soon the sails flapped above his head.

The wind caught the sails. The boat swung wildly round and the boom almost knocked him off the deck. He rushed for the helm and turned the boat into the wind.

The wind filled the sails and he felt the boat move, dancing over the sea. He was steering the boat and now he could decide which way to go!

Laughing, he turned the boat towards the misty shores and sailed away, free at last.

Part Three

Taking steps

Moccasins

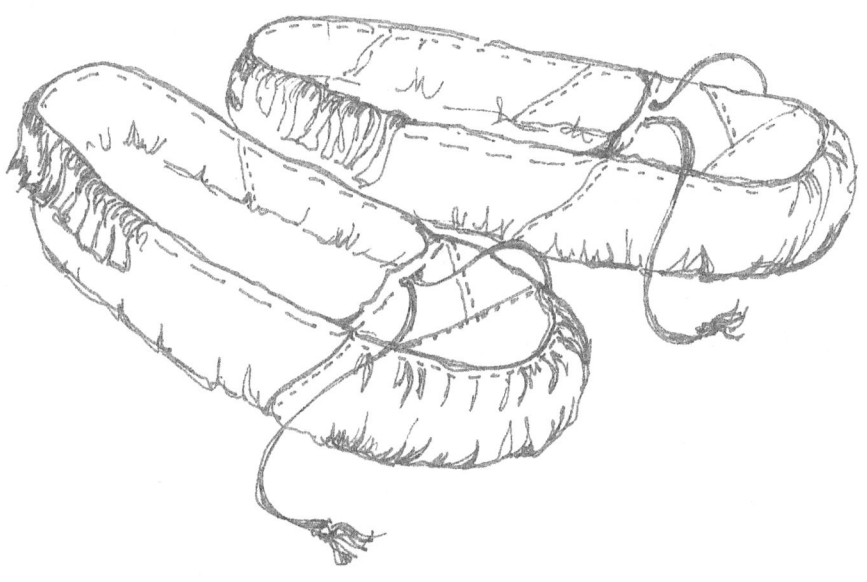

Carry out a creative and loving reappraisal of your past.......

I came to a place where I had left an old leather suitcase neglected in a corner. I imagined that there was great sadness left in it, that seemed to have something to do with me.

I leaned down and inspected the tattered leather, which I had slashed with a knife. I saw the damage I had done when I wrenched it open. I stroked the smooth leather surface, wondering what journeys that case had made that I could never know about.

I was lost for a long time, pondering the mysteries of the case. Then I saw that the leather was a warm, brown colour. It was soft and malleable. I knew at once what to do.

I took up my scissors and cut carefully into the leather until I had several pieces lying about my feet. I spent a long time carefully planning and placing the pieces this way and that.

Then I knew what I could make. I took up my needle and started to stitch. For many hours I worked, until my fingers were sore and my eyes ached.

I made a small rucksack and a pair of moccasins.

I saw the road stretching out ahead of me, inviting me to walk on.

I put the rucksack on my back, placed the moccasins on my feet, and set off, singing.

The Empty Box

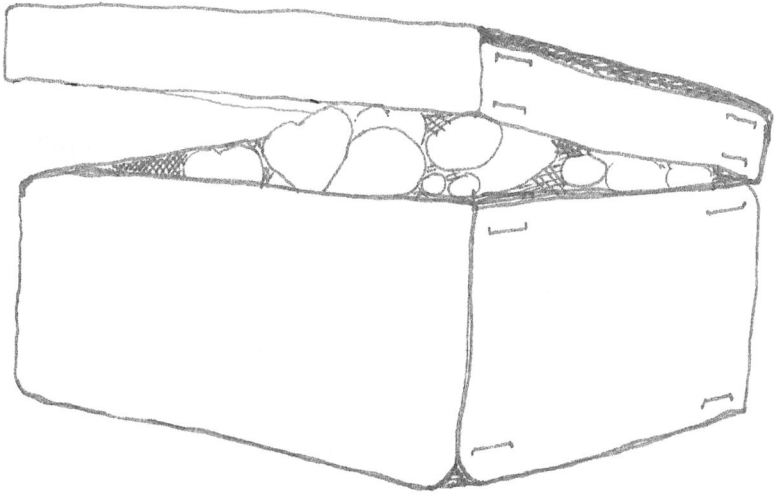

Recognise that love is everywhere, but invisible...

There once was a woman called Colette and she was having a birthday. Her best friend in all the world gave her a present.

It was a very ordinary cardboard box with a lid. As soon as she had it in her hand, it was clear to Colette that there was nothing in this box.

It felt very light. When her friend wasn't looking, she gave it a little shake to see if the thing inside was so soft and so light that you could hardly feel it. It was empty. Colette was bitterly disappointed and she put the box on the side and left it there.

Her friends kept asking, "When are you going to open your birthday present?" Colette didn't want to be hurt by proving that there was nothing in the box. She would rather keep the mystery of never quite knowing.

Time went by, and eventually Colette was ready to take the lid off the box. Her friends gathered around her. She put the box on her lap and she took off the lid.

It was not empty. It was absolutely full to overflowing with the love of her best friend.

As the lid came off, the love bubbled up over the side of the box. It spread over Colette, over her friends and into every corner of the room.

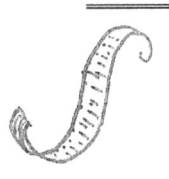 

Orthan's Herd

Own up to the fact that scapegoating is cowardly and irresponsible....

Once upon a time, in a land far away, there were two goats and their names were Ermey and Orthan. They were brothers. They grew up on the edge of the rocky desert, nibbling at all the green things that sprung up among the rocks. Their master, Eblis, was a good man and he looked after them well. They grew up from tiny little kids into strong goats. They were pure white and shaggy, as were all the goats who lived in the mountains around the city.

Eblis heard that the king needed two goats of purest white and they were to be taken to the palace for the annual ceremony of atonement. It had always been his dream that one day his goats would be the best and purest and they would be chosen to take part in the ceremony. So he washed Ermey and Orthan carefully, so their shaggy goats were purest white and their bright black eyes shone through their long manes.

Sure enough, when the spring came and the harvest was gathered, Eblis got his heart's desire: his goats were chosen.

Soon, it was time for his two goats to be taken to the palace. Eblis wore his best tunic of bright green and walked proudly with his wooden staff, right up to the door of the palace. Then a man in a purple robe led the goats away without a word. Eblis turned and went back to his herd, proud of his two little goats but wondering what was to become of them.

He walked slowly and thoughtfully back to the mountains and tended his herd, as he and his father had done for many years. He knew that there would be a moment of choice, where one would live and the other would die. He hoped in his secret

ORTHAN'S HERD

heart that the one to live would be Orthan, because there was a gentleness in his eyes that Ermey didn't have. Then he thought again and began to hope that Ermey would be the one to live, because there was a strength in him that was so full of life, that it must be expressed.

Meanwhile, in the palace yard, Elmey and Orthan were standing on a wooden dais, while people scrutinised them from every angle.

"Which is the perfect one?" they pondered.

Orthan thought, "Well, I know it's not me, because of the blemish on my throat. Ermey is free of any blemish. He is the perfect one."

Ermey was thinking, "They say that I am free of blemish but how can that be? Maybe I am perfect! Maybe I will be chosen."

Then the King came out of the palace and sat on his throne in the sun. The people were suddenly hushed. Ermey and Orthan stood, looking as handsome as they could, hoping that they would not let Eblis down in any way.

The king studied them for a long time. Then he stood up and came forward. The goats held their breath and he approached. The king's eyes were of the deepest blue and they looked kindly. The goats knew that they had no need to fear. Whichever way the choice went, this was a good man.

The king reached out his hand and touched Ermey. "This goat is without blemish. This goat is chosen."

The people cheered loudly and Ermey was lifted down from the dais and lead away. The two brothers, who had lived all their lives together until this moment, exchanged glances of farewell.

They did not know what was to happen, but they knew that they would never see each other again.

Orthan was left alone with a young boy, who lead him off the dais and took him out of the city to a clearing, where a few people were gathering. They had pieces of cloth and paper in their hands and some of them were carrying buckets and brushes.

There came a great shout from the city centre and a cry went up: "We offer his life in sacrifice of atonement!"

At once Orthan knew, with a great wrench in his heart, that his brother was dead. The goat without blemish, Ermey his brother, had been sacrificed. He, Orthan, was to live. For one terrible moment Orthan wanted to die too, rather than live on without his brother and know life without him.

He was too filled with grief and sorrow to notice that people were streaming out of the city towards him. He was too shaken to feel afraid of dying, or even of being approached by so many people.

Yet the people did not kill him. Rather, they spread some kind of sticky stuff all over his shaggy coat. Then they began to stick papers and pieces of cloth all over him until there was not a place on his coat that was not sticky and covered.

Orthan was puzzled. When would he too be sacrificed? When would he be killed like his brother? What was to happen to him, the white goat with the blemish on his throat? What punishment was he to endure for not being perfect enough? His black eyes were dull and sad. He stared at the rocky ground, not caring about the jeers and laughter of the people, who danced round him triumphantly.

ORTHAN'S HERD

Then he felt their sticks beating on his rump and he felt them moving him forward. They shoved him roughly, until he was stumbling down the path into the valley and over the hills towards the desert. The sun was hot but the people persisted. They beat him with sticks and threw stones at him, so that his head was bleeding.

He could hardly see where he was going. When evening came and the sun was setting, the people left him. By then he was deep into the desert. When Orthan moved to follow them (for he was born in a herd and accustomed to follow) they threw stones at him. So he learned to turn away and head off deep into the desert, where at least there were no more stones.

Soon, as darkness fell. The desert was once more empty and the sky was black overhead. Orthan was alone.

He did not understand. He did not know what he was to do. It seemed that he must stay in the desert away from people. He missed the herd. He missed Eblis. He felt itchy and sore along his back as the sticky stuff began to dry out.

He laid down on the ground and rolled in the dust, but the sticky stuff gathered up all the dust and made things worse. He shook himself and some of the dust flew off, but still the papers and the cloths stuck to him.

He was weary and he stumbled on, until he came to a tree where he lay down and rested until dawn.

The next day he searched for tiny green shoots but there were none. So he walked on, thirsty and looking for food. He became weaker and weaker. The sticky stuff dried in the hot sun and gradually the papers and the cloths fell off. He walked away from them, feeling the increasing lightness.

By the second day he was very weak and thirsty. He lay and dreamed of streams of water that would wash him white again and where he could drink and slake his thirst. But when he awoke there was nothing.

Orthan knew he must die. Not the glorious death of his brother, draped in purple with the crowds cheering but here in the desert, alone. Gradually he slipped deeper and deeper into death, until there were two breaths left to him and he knew he must die.

And a voice said; "Get up, Orthan! Come and drink."

There ahead of him was a great herd of goats of all shapes and sizes, calling him.

"Who are you?" he asked.

"We are the scapegoats of the past and the present," they told him. "Come and join us, and you will never be thirsty again."

Summoning up all the remaining strength he had, he rose to his feet, sustained by their voices. He came to them and drank, for there was a small pool of water round which they were gathered. Gradually, as he drank from the little pond and took the dry grasses that were in that place, he felt his strength return.

He looked around him and saw that the goats were of all ages, sizes and colours. Each one had a small blemish. They all showed him their blemish and spoke of it with pride.

"But I have blemish too!" he said gladly. He lifted up his head to show the blemish at his throat. They all stared at the blemish and admired it. Orthan was very glad that to have a

ORTHAN'S HERD

blemish was a good thing here in the dessert. In his birth herd, this tiny blemish had always been the biggest difficulty in his life. He wondered how this herd of goats would feel if Ermey were to appear among them, with his pure white coat, free of any blemish.

Soon he discovered that every one of these goats had a brother or sister who had been sacrificed in the same way as Ermey. He was puzzled, so he asked the oldest and wisest goat what it could all mean.

"We are the scapegoats, who bear away the sins of the people," he said. "The papers and cloths represented the sins of the people. They stuck them all over you and sent you out into the desert. It has been the same for everyone."

"But how could the King do this to us?" asked Orthan. "He is a good and kindly man and surely he would not want to hurt us."

The other goats looked sad. "We are the sin bearers," he said. "It is our work, our destiny. We do it because we must. People cannot carry their own sin and shame, so we must do it for them."

Orthan was angry. He didn't like the desert, where there was little to eat except for a few dried grasses. He hated the dirty water of the pool and yearned for the clear stream where his birth herd always drank.

He watched and wondered for a long time and then he decided. He went back to the wise old goat and said, "I want to go back."

"You can't, I'm afraid. You can't go back now. You must live out the rest of your life in the desert."

Orthan was angry. "I will not!" he cried. "Who is coming with me? I am going!"

The wise old goat looked very sorrowful. There was nothing he could do. There were several goats who wanted to go back. One by one they set off, trailing slowly down the desert path without a backward glance. They had made a new herd: Orthan's herd.

They walked for many days across the desert until they saw the city on the hilltop. There were more things to eat now, and they were feeling stronger with every step. They came to the hills near the city and sure enough, here was Eblis with his herd.

He looked at Orthan and stared and stared. Then he screamed and ran away, taking his herd with him. Orthan stood with his own herd, hardly able to believe that the man who had cared for him all his life would not speak to him.

So it was that Orthan's herd went from place to place near that city and everywhere they were shunned.

Orthan grew very angry. He began to kick at the little fences that the people had built, and turn over the stalls in the market place. The whole herd jumped over the fields and gardens and trampled on the chickens who squarked and flew upwards in a shower of feathers.

"We will not be shunned!" cried Orthan's herd.

"We will be heard!" they shouted, as they chased the children.

"We will be accepted like any other goats!" said Orthan, as he bit into the women's skirts.

ORTHAN'S HERD

Eventually, the people turned on them and they were rounded up into a corral.

The people watched them standing there, glaring back at them with angry black eyes. The children and the other goat herds came down from the hilltops to stare at this strange, new herd of goats that had come so suddenly out of the desert and were destroying everything in sight.

Orthan felt very sad and sorry that he had broken the fences and bitten the woman's skirt. He looked with his bright, black eyes straight into the eyes of a young boy who had come to stare at them, for the boy had bright blue eyes, just like the king.

The boy said: "This is the one." The people were suddenly silent.

"This is the one I want," the boy said.

All at once, there was a commotion in the corner of the courtyard. The king entered. The boy ran up to him and was gathered up into his arms. This was the king's son and they both looked at each other with a look of perfect love.

"Father, I know which one I want - that one, with a blemish on his throat. He will be mine."

"My son, you shall have him. Go and get him from the herd."

The people were afraid. "My Lord! Do not send your son into this herd! They are terrible and they destroy everything. They will destroy him!"

"No. They won't," said the king. "Go!" he said to the little prince.

"Will I be safe, Father?" The boy looked a little frightened by what the people had said.

"You will be safe if you look on them with kindness," said the king.

So the boy kept his blue eyes fixed upon Orthan's bright black eyes, with the same look of great kindness that he had learned from his father.

He came through the gate into the corral. The goats shifted around him as he made his way through the herd. None of the goats did anything to harm the boy. Then the boy and the goat stood face to face and eye to eye.

"Come with me," said the boy. Turning, he led the way out of the corral and through the gate without looking back. Orthan followed him, as he had always followed Eblis and would follow any man who had kindness in his eyes.

As they did this, the people whispered to themselves, "This is a miracle!"

The king then said, "Release them."

The people removed the wattles and the herd stood quietly in the courtyard, free and un-penned.

After a few moments of silence, a woman approached the herd. She walked up to a big black goat and touched him.

"Come with me," she said and led him away into the hills.

One by one, the people came with kindness, each to claim one goat. Without laying a hand on them, they led them away to the green pastures which lay waiting for them, with clear streams to drink from.

Orthan lived in the king's palace for the rest of his days. He often thought of his brother and missed him terribly, but when the prince came to stroke his shaggy coat and rest his head against his neck, he knew that life was good.

Hiding in the Light

Realise that you are not invisible...

I stood still in that place where they were, and it was dark. I was afraid to move. I heard voices and they seemed to be talking to me, but I could not be sure, so I smiled, just in case. I found my way about by guesswork. I made my own torches to light the way, woven from my hair and spittle, until my mouth was dry, my hair was thin and my scalp was a weeping sore.

It was so lonely and silent there that I looked for others who shared the place with me. I heard their voices speaking to each other. I spoke to them about their thoughts and dreams and they spoke to me. It was less lonely then.

They spoke to me about another place where it was not dark and they did not have to use their hair and spittle to make torches, for the light shone always. I wanted to be in that place.

They seemed so confident and sure of themselves, moving about with ease, not needing to guess where they were but somehow knowing. This puzzled me and I did not understand.

Then one day there was someone who saw me, and he said so. I was amazed, for how could he know I was there in the dark? I couldn't see him, so how could he see me? I could only see what I could work out from what he told me, his tone of voice and how he made me feel.

Surely he could only see what he imagined me to be? I wasn't sure he was all that accurate in his guessing, for he seemed to stumble about in the dark and hold on tight to anything he fell over. He fell over me several times and often bruised me in the process.

Then there was another person who agreed to be my friend and help me explore the place where I lived and learn more about

it. I hoped that she would guide me, but she always waited for me to find the way and then she would follow. This made me afraid at first but soon I learned to guess what she wanted and went the way she seemed to like best.

We met many times by agreement, until it seemed to me that somehow she could truly see me there in the dark, but I did not understand how. I longed for her to prove to me that I could be seen and heard. I dared to ask her to reach out and touch me, so I could know she had really seen me. She refused to touch me. I was even more afraid, and asked her more and more urgently, "Touch me! Please touch me! Then I can know where I am and where you are and feel safe here in the dark. Then I will have someone to hold on to."

Still she refused to touch me. I wept, wailed and sulked. I shouted that she was wicked to refuse me this simple thing - just to bother to reach out for me, to show she cared about me! Still she waited for me to do something but she never said what.

I reflected upon this and realised that for me to be touched was very painful! The wounds had been hidden for so long that they had festered.

I felt the wound that I had inflicted upon myself and felt sorry that I had not taken care of my skin and allowed it to heal. How I needed healing balm now, and loving care to heal the wounds that now felt so raw!

I cried out for help and care - I longed for someone to give me a healing touch to make things better. I lay there in pain and no one came to me. I longed for someone to care enough to reach out to me. No one noticed. No one cared enough about

me to reach out to me in my pain.

Then I took my pain, which had begun to heal a little, to my friend. I told her how it was that no one came to me and no one cared. I wanted so much for her to reach out to me. I wept when I told her this, for I knew that she would not reach out to me - but at least there was kindness in her voice and she did not turn away.

In her kindness I saw that she understood how much it hurt that no one came to me in my pain. I saw her understanding, and I knew then that I saw her.

I knew that at last there was a light to see by and surely she was making it! I tried to thank her for making the light, so I could see. She did not want my thanks. She said it seemed that I had made the light for myself. But how could I have made the light for myself? I had not made a torch for a long time, for my scalp was too sore, my hair was thin and my mouth too dry.

I looked about me and saw clearly. I saw the faces of those around me. I saw them and knew they saw me, for the world was lit from end to end.

I had found the light by simply opening my eyes.

Sisyphus Unbound

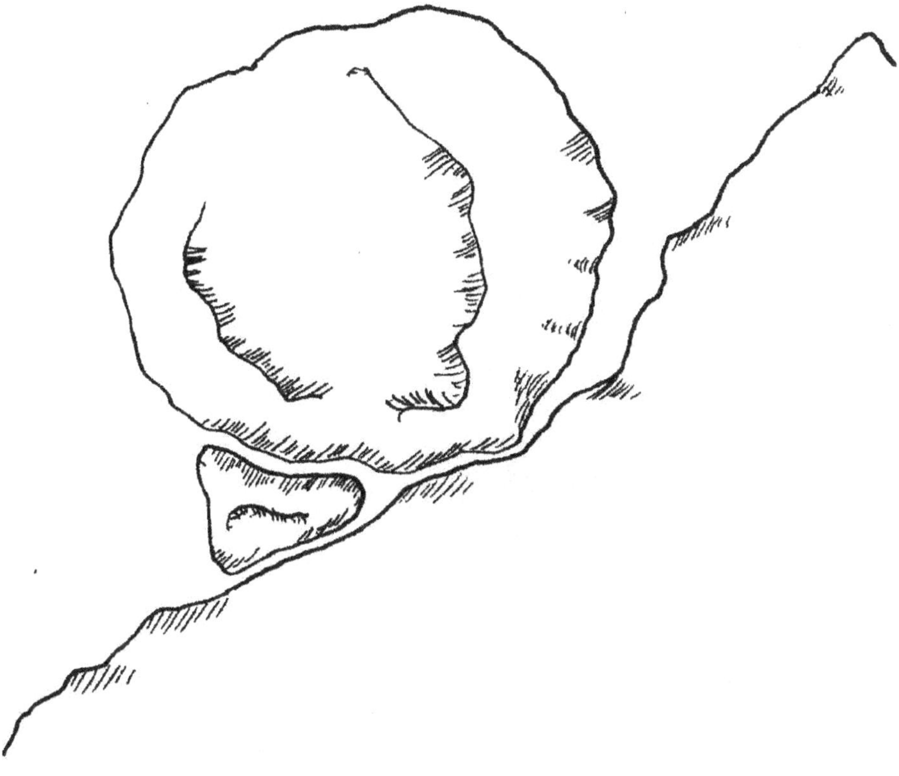

Understand that whatever happens and however helpless you may feel, all the choices are there, all of the time...

The hill was rugged and steep and the narrow path well-worn, for the man with the stone had pushed his way uphill many times. He was tall and muscular with strong arms and legs. He sweated as he rolled the stone higher and higher, up the path towards the summit. The day wore on as he struggled on alone, step by painful step, ever upwards, slowly but surely, inch by inch. Within a few yards of the top, he slipped, and his feet slithered on the wet ground. The stone slipped from his grasp and it began a slow descent, gathering speed as it went.

This man Sisyphus had once been a king. He was clever. He used his wits to rule and ruled well with an iron hand. Yet when Death came to claim him, he seemed to be powerless. However, Sisyphus had already worked out a plan to cheat Death. Sisyphus had left him chained to the wall at the gates of Hades - in chains that had been designed for Sisyphus himself.

The price of this cunning was that Death cursed Sisyphus with an endless, fruitless task - to push a huge stone up and over the mountain. Soon it was clear that without help Sisyphus would never reach the top and never see the stone roll over the summit and down the other side, thus setting him free from the curse. He knew he needed a friend.

The first friend he called upon was Hope.

"Just keep trying," cried Hope, as Sisyphus strained to move the heavy stone. "The summit is not far, and you are strong. You can do this; never give up. Keep hoping that tomorrow it will be better, that the stone will not seem so heavy and will move easily. Soon your curse will be broken and you will be free. Keep cheerful and keep believing that this can be done!"

With the help of Hope, Sisyphus pushed the stone to the top with renewed strength, but again he slipped up and the stone rolled downwards into the valley with a great crash.

At the bottom Despair was waiting for him, as he always did, laughing.

"See how weak you are!" said Despair, in his dark, crackling voice. "You will never do it, you will be condemned to this fate for the rest of eternity. And I will be here to watch you and laugh at your weakness."

Sisyphus gathered his strength once more. He refused to hear the cracking laughter from the valley but set his heart and mind upon that summit, which was so far away and unreachable.

Halfway up the mountain, with the stone already quite a good way up, Sisyphus called upon Love to help him place a wedge under the stone. There on the mountainside, with the stone still and firm and the path stretching out before and behind him, he rested and gathered his strength once more for the journey upwards. As he rested, he heard voices calling to him.

"Run away!" cried Freedom. "Do not try any more! The stone is too big for you. Run now while you have the chance!"

"Stay here." said Responsibility. "This is your task. Until it is completed you will never be freed from this curse."

"You don't have to do this," said Choice. "Things do not have to be this way."

The chattering and arguing went on and on. Sisyphus tried to listen to them and hear their reasoning. As he rested, he applied all his own wits to try and solve the puzzle of what he must do next. Soon, the wedge that Love had helped him put in place was no longer strong enough to hold the stone. It rolled back down the mountain.

Sisyphus plodded slowly down the mountainside to meet Despair, who was laughing as usual.

"Listen to what I have to say," said Despair.

"You know that I will never listen to you!" cried Sisyphus. "You sap all my strength and I cannot move the stone if I hear you."

"But listen just this once," said Hope, who was standing by his side as usual.

"You may be able to learn from him," said Love, standing a little way off but near enough to provide some encouragement.

So Sisyphus listened to Despair, and this is what he was told: Death had been discussing with Despair how Death might be released to do his work. Together they had created a bargain. However, Despair said that Death would only tell Sisyphus of the bargain face to face and not through a messenger.

So leaving the stone behind him, Sisyphus went to the door of Hades, where Death was chained with the chains Sisyphus himself had placed there.

"Release me to do my work," said Death, "and I will use these chains to help you to pull the stone up and over the hill. With these chains and my strength, we can work together. Soon your task will be done!"

Sisyphus knew that once Death was unchained, his life would be once more in danger. So he took the chains and fastened Death to the stone with them and told Death to help him to push the stone.

Despair came with them. His derisory laughter and Death's cold hand did little to spur him on. His strength was so small and weak, that the stone soon slipped back into the valley. He stood exhausted and watched as Death went rolling down the hill, over and over, with the chains wrapped more and more tightly around him. Sisyphus could hear Despair laughing in triumph as always.

Sisyphus slumped down onto the path. There below him in the valley was the stone, with Death chained to it. Despair was looking on. Sisyphus stared at them for a long time. He did not want to go so close to Death again.

Then he heard the voice of Choice calling him. "Now is your chance to act, to set yourself free!" Before him, Choice revealed another path that he had not seen before.

It led into the unknown, but while Death lay in the valley chained to the stone, Sisyphus could now take this path and be free, until Death caught up with him once more.

Looking neither at the unreachable summit of the mountain nor the familiar depths of despair, Sisyphus set out along the new path, taking with him Hope and Love to help him on his way.

The Door

Learn that healing cannot be rushed. It can only be allowed....

The wall before me was covered in thick ivy that had grown over the years. The ivy was strong and the leaves very green. Yet there was just a hint, in the shape of the green covering, that suggested there may be something behind it. Bit by bit, I tore off the resisting stems until the red, crumbling bricks of the wall were revealed.

I searched for many years, tearing away the ivy which, neglected, soon grew again. Then one day I noticed that there was wood beneath the ivy. As I carefully took off the leaves and stems, I saw that it was a wooden structure - it was a door.

I examined the door, noticing the strong wood panels, the square strong frame, the veins of the deep oak wood. There was no doorknob, no keyhole and no key. The door stood in the wall, mute and mysterious. Why was it there? What was on the other side? Would I ever be able to open it?

I asked a friend to help me. Together we cleared away the remainder of the ivy. I explored with my fingernails the crack around the door. I put my ear close, so close to the wood and listened as hard as I could. I thought I could hear something but it was only the beating of my own heart.

Together my friend and I debated why the door was there and what may be on the other side. I sat there for many days staring at the door, dreaming of the day when I might know how to open it and know what was there on the other side.

In my dream, a man stood in the open doorway. How was it that the door had opened? Beyond the tall figure of the man, there was a strange landscape that I thought I knew, but I woke up and the dream faded from my memory, leaving only a sense of loss and isolation.

I grew angry at the mute and silent square shape of the door. I threw myself against it and beat upon it with my fists. I knew that if I could only open the door, then I would know what was on the other side.

I could not go on with my life until I saw that strange landscape that my heart already knew about but my mind could not encompass.

I was obsessed. I fell to the ground and wept at the injustice of it - that the door should be revealed to me so clearly, but I was unable to see it or share in it. I knew that there were people on the other side of the door.

I knew that, if I could only pass through that enigmatic space, I would be united with those people. I felt a deep sense that only in that passing through would I be able to taste true happiness.

The days passed. I raged and wept by turns. Gradually I sank into despair, as I waited and waited for some inspiration that would tell me how to open the door. The door looked like such a thin plank of wood, but it was impenetrable and shut tight.

It was not locked against me, for there was no key. It was simply sealed by a force that I did not understand. It did not yield to my strivings, however strong or subtle I tried to be with it. My heart was breaking and my mood was blackened by the sense of being denied the mystery.

Then one day my heart did break and I was left lying in hopelessness. I was filled with fear that I would never pass beyond the door; that my life would be over and I would never taste the joy and fulfilment that I knew was beyond that door.

As I lay, I stared at the ground beneath the door. I touched the soft earth. I realised that I was unable to see the bottom of the door, for the earth had piled up against it and grass had grown in and under it.

I reached out with a feeble grip and scraped gently at the earth, taking away any obstruction that may stop me glimpsing through the crack beneath the door. When I had scraped away enough, I saw that there was no crack, no space to give a glimpse - just the mute and silent wooden face of the door, waiting for me. What was I to do?

I lay there in my broken-heartedness and thought and dreamed. I asked my heart why it had broken. What terrible hurt had broken it? And my heart answered that I had broken it myself in my striving. I had not learned to wait for the door itself to tell me what to do.

So privately, when no one was looking, I asked the door what I should do, feeling foolish to be doing such a thing. As I did this, my heart leaped with joy.

I knew what to do. I was to scrape away all the debris that lay on my side of the door, to make the way clear for it to open, for it was going to open towards me!

I leapt to my feet with renewed energy. I scraped with all my might and main to make a way clear for the door to open. Then I sat down to watch and wait.

I waited for a long, long time. I grew angry at the long time I was being asked to wait. I raged at the door, asking, begging it to

THE DOOR

open. Surely this had been my life's work - to find the door and to make it possible to see on the other side? What more must I do to open this door?

So once more, I turned to the door and asked in my heart for guidance, for I knew a great longing and I did not know what I must do. I knelt before the door, no longer raging, not begging but simply asking for the door to tell me what I must do. I knelt in silence listening but no answer came.

It was hard to hear because of the noise behind me. There were people behind me and I wondered what they were doing.

So I turned to see what was going on. My friends were laughing and singing and holding out their hands to me, so I went to join them and felt their loving presence.

Somehow, although I did not look behind me, I knew that this is what the door was telling me in my heart: that I should be with my friends and live my life day by day.

Then I knew at last that, if I stopped trying to open it, one day, when it was ready, the door would simply swing open towards me and let me in.

With that sure knowledge I set off on the many pathways that lay before me. My heart was filled with joy, for I knew that, when the time was right, the door would simply be open when I turned to look.

Then I would be free at last to pass through into the place on the other side.

The Key

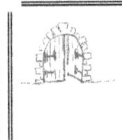

*One day soon, you will find the key to your future.
Keep looking, it is there....*

I awoke and opened my eyes at last. I looked about me in the gloom. I could see the soft bed, the warm enclosing walls and the high window. The bed was warm as I lay on it and dreamed many dreams where I was falling, skating downhill, missing trains and trying not to drown. The high window was beyond the reach of my gaze. I often wondered what I would see if I looked out, but I didn't.

The prison was small but there was enough for my needs. I had my books and the TV, and some pencils to write with. I read stories, wrote stories and told stories to my friends who were there on the other side of the wall. Sometimes I wished I could see my friends clearly but always there was the wall between us.

Then there was a crashing and screaming. I did not want to hear, to see, or be seen. I stayed silently inside my warm prison, glad that I did not have to be involved. For many years the crashing went on, and when it was silent I waited for it to begin again.

Then there was a long silence. I waited, imagining what may be going on in that silence, what terrible things were being planned against me. But gradually I begun to wonder if the silence was simply silence, and nothing to be feared?

I noticed the door. It was in the gloomiest corner, and it was closed. I lay in bed and wondered what lay beyond the door. I stared at that door for a long time and heard gentle voices outside.

One day they called to me, with soft tones and whispered words that I did not let myself hear, for outside the door was terror and mayhem and chaos! I was safer here inside my

THE KEY

familiar prison with its comforts and warmth!

The voices outside the door became louder and more insistent. I heard some angry voices saying I must come out, and other voices saying they understood why I felt I had to stay inside. I heard songs and stories that were not quite distinct and the voices of people I loved and wanted to be near to.

I began to want to open the door! I walked right up to it, dared to touch it, dared to see its outlines and the way it was closed against me. I raged against the door, against the smallness of my prison space! I knew that there were others outside, unafraid. If the door would only open, I could be with them. I began to speak to them about the door, about how it felt to be locked in, unable to get out.

They were waiting for me to do something but they never said what. I knew I must do something but I didn't know what. There was no one to tell me how! I became very angry that I had never been shown the way out of this door!

I was terribly lonely in my tiny cell. The stories lost their appeal: they were a place to escape to but they were not real freedom. How I longed for freedom! I longed to be out there with all the others - able to feel part of them, be with them, feel the warmth of their presence and really get to know them.

Again, I raged against the door, flailing against it with my fists, weeping and crying. I raged endlessly against the fact that I had to be in this tiny prison, where the air was dank and the window so small.

One day I became aware of soft voices speaking to me: - the same words again and again. I was afraid of what they were saying, and blocked my ears to their words. They were saying,

"Open the door! Open the door!"

I did not after all want to open that door, because I was afraid of being outside where I didn't know how to behave, or how to be myself.

Gradually I learned to listen to the voices, because I came to understand that they were my friends, that they wished me no harm. As they spoke to me gently, I came nearer and nearer to the door, until I could place my hand on it and feel the cold steel of the latch under my hand.

After many days, I put my hand upon the latch and dared to turn it. I was very afraid but the soft voices continued, insisting that it was safe, and that I was held in mind while I tried to do this thing. I dared to push. I pushed with all my strength against the door but it resisted. It was locked.

Then I became truly enraged. How could they do this to me! How could they lead me to believe that I could open this door! How can anyone open a door that is locked? They were stupid; they had let me down! They were evil, exploiting my wish to escape; planting ideas of freedom in my head that I could never have!

I sulked for a long time. I wouldn't listen. I lay in my bed and returned to my dreams, but they had a different quality now. They were about walls, bars, fences and barriers. I longed to get out but I couldn't. How I longed to be free!

Some days later, at the high window, I heard someone singing. The song got into my heart and woke me up from my dream. It was a song about a key - it lay in a dark corner for years and years but was found at last. How I wished that someone would come and help me find that key!

THE KEY

How I wished that I could be found - that someone would come and find me in my tiny cell and set me free! Yet in the deep places of my heart there was gladness that no one had come - that I had not been found. Were I to be found, I would have to go out into that fearful place where people may try to exploit me again.

Then one day I saw the key, there in the corner of the room. I wondered how I had never seen it before. Perhaps I had seen it, but ignored it.

It was hard for me, picking up that key. I waited a long time before I even touched it. All the time I held it, I sang the song to myself, about the key that can open the door.

I could not remember locking the door, but perhaps someone had locked it for me, believing that it would keep me safe. Maybe my mother had been here in this prison. Perhaps I had been born into the prison and had known no other life.

I did place the key in the lock. I did turn it.

I opened the door and stepped out into the arms of those who had waited for me so patiently.

Without them, without their encouraging words - understanding my hesitation, understanding my fear, gently letting me feel my own power to decide - I could never have done it.

Beyond the Wire

Notice how your fear of freedom keeps you trapped....

I stood in an unfamiliar place, where I needed to hold tight to those who had brought me there. The ground was smooth and there were huge open areas, and I could stretch and run and grow stronger every day. I saw the sky, the clouds and all the people around me, also running and growing stronger, smiling with the joy of being free!

For a long, long time I played there in this space, with the hard, smooth ground secure beneath my feet and the high, blue sky above my head. As I grew stronger I wandered about in that place to find the limits of it. No one spoke very much about the outer limits, except for dark hints and sideways glances.

Then one day I saw the perimeter. It was made of barbed wire, in a terrible tangled mess, all around the edge of the space where I was. The wire was strong and twisted. The barbs were cruel and spiky. I did not dare to touch the wire lest my skin be torn.

I simply stared at it for a long time. The wire was so thick it was very difficult to see what may be outside and I was filled with fear at the prospect of what may lie beyond. I became afraid of looking outwards. Instead looked inwards, to the space where I was growing stronger every day.

I was able to look back to my former prison in the centre of the space and realised that I was now in the prison compound. The floor made of was smooth concrete: it was not living earth.

Again I was trapped, even though there was plenty of space and people were happily playing, living their lives there in the compound, each trying not to think about what might lie beyond the edge.

BEYOND THE WIRE

I listened every day for a voice from beyond the wire. I yearned to hear a song; a story to encourage me; a voice to draw me onward, outwards towards the wire. I watched and thought, and calculated what to do.

There were three ways to get past this barrier: first I could lay a ladder against it and climb over, but where was the person to provide the ladder on the other side? There was no one there.

I decided to tunnel beneath it, and this seemed a good idea. I worked hard for many months to dig a secret tunnel under the wire; hoping that if I dug up enough dirt there would be a clear way through. But strangely, (or perhaps not so strangely, for I was afraid), the tunnel kept collapsing, and the more I dug the more I was trapped in the tunnel, away from the fresh air.

It was late evening when I found the wire cutters. They lay on the ground, available for anyone who noticed them to pick up. At once I knew that they were for me.

I would cut the wire, strand by strand, until I had made a smooth path through! I would allow others to come through with me and we could be all together in the place beyond the wire! I held the cutters close to me all night long, dreaming and wondering how I would see my way, for beyond the wire was a place with very little light.

In the early morning, I used all my wisdom to create a small torch. I lit it. In the dark before dawn I stepped out boldly across the compound towards the wire.

The wire loomed over me and I was afraid, but I kept walking and stretched out my hand towards the wire. I was prepared to risk tearing my skin and bleeding badly, if I could only be free!

I held up the wire cutters as a talisman before me. To my surprise, the wire gave way under my hand. As I walked into it, it began to dissolve away. Then I knew the truth - that I had made the barbs on the wire out of my pain and the wire was meshing me into my old, imprisoned life.

I simply stepped through, now understanding that I had made the wire out of my fear of freedom. Now I was making my own way through the space where I had imagined the wire to be.

I held up the torch I had made. Its tiny light showed me the road a little way before me into the dark.

As I stepped forward into my future, I felt hands upon me that were familiar, but which I could not see. Their gentle touch was enough for me to contain my fear and walk on.

Out of the Box

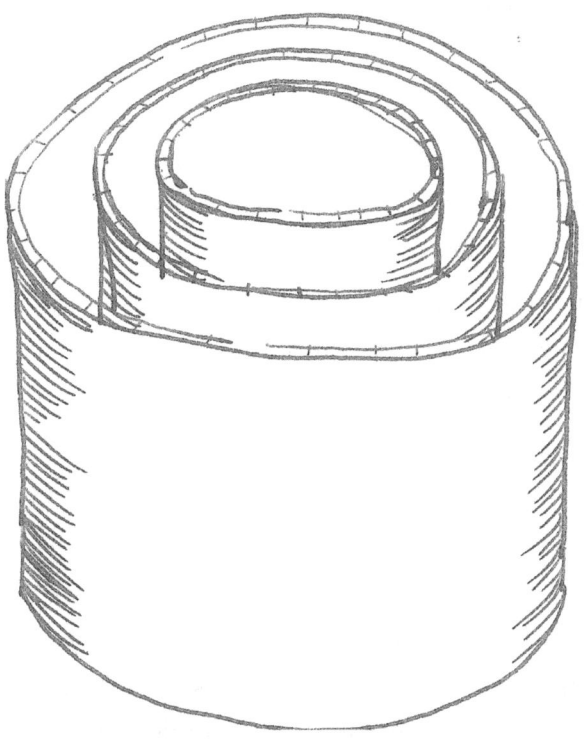

Time to let go of the past and become the person you were always meant to be....

I was in a place of complete darkness. It was a place I knew well and yet I was visiting it with my awareness for the first time. I opened my inner eye of awareness and saw a set of Chinese boxes, made of dark, dark wood with one packed inside the other.

I was where I had always been: in the outermost box, hemmed in on both sides, but I did not care. I could manage this for a lifetime. I was resigned to never being let out or escaping, in fact I had long since given up on the possibility of escaping. I settled for what I had. I was content. I was alone.

Yet somewhere, faintly sounding in the back of my mind, I heard a child cry out. Something deep in my heart awoke and responded to that cry.

I began to listen carefully to that tiny little voice. It seemed to be coming from the other side of the wall. My listening drew me inwards, to wonder about what was on the other side of the dark, inner wall of my prison. I realised that in the place where I was all I had ever managed to do was to walk in circles.

If I stopped walking round and made a hole in the wall, what would I find there? I made a very tiny hole in the wall and dared to look through. It was very dark there and it was filled with fear. I feared that I was stepping into a void; that I would vanish from the world and never find that little voice.

The voice sounded a little louder. In my heart I knew the child was lost and alone in the dark. I felt very sad that this lonely little child had no friend to comfort him.

So I stepped into the dark and fearful place to be near to and comfort the child. I did not know where I was or what to do. I felt helpless and sad that the child was lonely in his box

and I in mine. I realised then that I did not wish to be alone.

I walked round in that new space, which was much smaller than my former prison. Very soon I came back to where I had started walking. Round and round I walked, many, many times, but there was no way out. The child was still crying and alone. I grieved for that child and also felt sad to be alone.

I began to wonder how this thing had come about. Why I was sad and alone and grieving for a little child, who cried out endlessly in the dark but no one came? I wondered who the child was, and why I had always been alone.

I wondered if the child and I could be friends. I wanted to shout out but I had no voice.

I was left in silence with only the sound of the child's cry to guide me. Then I realised that the silence was all around me. The child's cry had stopped for he had given up in despair. I tried desperately to call out and found an unaccustomed voice of my own. I cried out in a whispery tone: "Where are you? Why will you not talk to me? I want to be your friend! "

There was only silence. There in my dark wooden prison, I felt more alone than ever. The silence of that child's cry spoke to me of the death of hope. My heart broke open at last.

The pain was terrible. I was racked with it. I clutched at my own body as I knew the pain of true desire at last. Out of that desire came rage and power. I would have what I wanted! I took my rage and power and smashed the wooden walls of my prison until they lay about me like matchwood.

I moved towards the centre, into the silence where the child had been. There was no sign of the child. He was gone.

The wind blew gently around me and I knew freedom, but

there was no one there, only myself, staring into the ruins of my wooden prison.

So I piled up all the wood and made it into a great beacon and lit with the new fire of life that was burning in me. The flames leapt high and the light of the beacon shone out over all the land.

In a distant place where he had been waiting all these long years, a child saw the light I had made and came home.

www.ingramcontent.com/pod-product-compliance
Lightning Source LLC
Chambersburg PA
CBHW031354040426
42444CB00005B/286